HOW
TO
DIE

Books also by Joshua Porter

The Great Georgia Dirt Dragon

With All Its Teeth: Sex, Violence, Profanity, and
the Death of Christian Art

Death to Deconstruction: Reclaiming Faithfulness
as an Act of Rebellion

Punk Rock vs. the Lizard People

HOW TO DIE

Joshua S. Porter

Chaos, Mortality, and the Scandal of Christian Discipleship

150 YEARS STRONG

DAVID C COOK

HOW TO DIE: CHAOS, MORTALITY, AND THE
SCANDAL OF CHRISTIAN DISCIPLESHIP
Published by David C Cook
4050 Lee Vance Drive
Colorado Springs, CO 80918 U.S.A.

Integrity Music Limited, a Division of David C Cook
Brighton, East Sussex BN1 2RE, England

DAVID C COOK®, the graphic circle C logo, and related marks
are registered trademarks of David C Cook.

Details in some stories have been changed to protect
the identities of the persons involved.

Unless otherwise noted, all Scripture quotations are taken from the Holy
Bible New International Version®, NIV®. Copyright © 1973, 2011 by Biblica,
Inc.™ Used by permission of Zondervan. All rights reserved worldwide. www.
zondervan.com. The "NIV" and "New International Version" are trademarks
registered in the United States Patent and Trademark Office by Biblica,
Inc.™ The author has added italics to Scripture quotations for emphasis.

Library of Congress Control Number 2024951609
ISBN 978-0-8307-8789-0
eISBN 978-0-8307-8790-6

© 2025 Joshua S. Porter
This book is represented by MacGregor & Luedeke Collaborative LLC.

The Team: Michael Covington, Kevin Scott, Gina
Pottenger, Leigh Davidson, Karen Sherry
Cover Design: Brian Mellema

Printed in the United States of America
First Edition 2025

1 2 3 4 5 6 7 8 9 10

070125

For Arlo.
Follow my example, as I follow
the example of Christ.

"Thus it begins; the cross is not the terrible end to an otherwise god-fearing and happy life, but it meets us at the beginning of our communion with Christ. When Christ calls a man, he bids him come and die."

DIETRICH BONHOEFFER (dead), *The Cost of Discipleship*

"This book belongs to the very few."

FRIEDRICH NIETZSCHE (also dead), *The Antichrist*

CONTENTS

How to Read this Book 11
Prologue 13
A Note from the Author 15

BOOK ONE: RUINER
Parable 25
I. First, the Entire Story in Summation 29
II.–III. Then, Three Distinct but Related Stories
　　Important for Understanding the Whole 49
IV. A Brief History of the Movement So Far 71
V.–VI. Finally, Some Things Christians Believe
　　as a Result 89
Another Parable 97

BOOK TWO: THE HARROWING OF HELL
Parable 107
A Note from the Author 109
I.–XVIII. The Master's Teaching 113

BOOK THREE: THE MANUAL OF DISCIPLINES
The Armamentarium 191
A Note from the Author 193
I.–VIII. The Master's Practices 199
IX. A Brief Word on the End 239
Final Note from the Author 243
Disciple's Vow 249
Final Parable 251
Epilogue 261

Acknowledgments 269

HOW TO READ THIS BOOK

WHAT FOLLOWS IS DESIGNED as a spiritual odyssey, not a linear collection of information-driven essays. This supplemental handbook for discipleship consists of stories, manuals, poetry, and prose. Varying passages can and should be read at alternating tempos according to genre and serve the reader best when revisited and reconsidered along the journey of reading.

PROLOGUE: WHEN THE GARDEN WAS RUINED

WHY ARE PEOPLE TERRIBLE? I look out the window and sigh. The garden is ruined. All along the rutted topography of carefully plotted bulbs, sprouting in symmetry, bright green against the puckering soil, there grow long, invasive stalks, hatching spiderlike from the earth. I think, *The gardener is going to hit the ceiling.* But when he sees it, his expression remains unchanged. It's like he expected this.

"We set the whole thing up exactly like you wanted," I say. "How'd it get like this? Where did the weeds come from?"

"Someone was trying to ruin it," he answers.

"I'll go," I assure him, pushing my feet into boots. "I'll pull them up before things get out of control."

Then his hand is on my shoulder. Gentle pressure. "Wait," he says, nodding out the window at the garden. "You might pull the plants up by mistake. Leave them."

"So that's it? The garden is ruined?"

"No. Let them grow together. When it's time to harvest, we'll separate the good stuff from the bad. We'll do away with everything that isn't as it should be. When the time comes, we'll sort it out."

"So, what, then? We just wait?"

"No. There's work to do," he says. He walks out the door toward the garden, his sleeves rolled, his hands eager for the dirt.

LOCUST SHELLS

ALL OF LIVING IS a series of deaths. We endure these deaths—one after the other—and we become something different than what we were before we died, like a cicada straining up and out of the split seam of its own exoskeleton, the old self little more than a brittle husk. This ritual of hatching can be beautiful or grotesque—depends on who you ask.

Somewhere else in the world—some other time and place—a human skeleton was discovered in the darkness of a cave. It was fettered in chains, this skeleton, and in a life long ago, the man to whom the skeleton belonged had burrowed into a great yawning mouth in the earth to expedite the dying process. What did it see down in that cave, this skeleton, when it was robed in flesh, before time stripped it naked, leaving only bones and chains for academics and photographers and writers? I saw a picture of the skeleton in a library as I was fanning the pages of a university volume on religion. I looked at it for a while, scratching the side of my face under the sickly white glow of fluorescent bulbs. A few feet away, a man took an audible sip of coffee from a branded paper cup and cleared his throat. I wondered, *Is this what he, the skeleton, had in mind?*

I doubt God smiled his approval on that starving skeleton in the dark or that he asked the monk to whom the skeleton belonged to bear chains, to be alone, or to offer such a display of allegiance as to wither and rot just to prove it so, his chains and bones eventually becoming a magazine clipping, a textbook entry—"See Fig. A." Perhaps God asked of the monk the love that burns away sin and rotates the wayward heart, but maybe cold discipline was all the skeleton had to offer, so he clung to those stones and those chains like the cicada to the branch, waiting, straining to peel free of himself. Maybe he closed his eyes, wanting to will some other, better version of himself to escape the not-so-great one. Maybe he was down there in the dark, that monk, waiting for something to happen, not knowing that the something that would happen would be death. All of living is a series of deaths.

The entire world is organized and configured for the destruction of the religious imagination. Our inborn appetites for the mysterious, the mystic, the something behind and beyond all this have been dulled by touchscreens and fast food and same-day deliveries, and we are left with little more than the sad, stunted superstition that the universe is mostly quantifiable and totally without grand design or purpose. The world, as we know it, is a series of flashing images, of twinkling distractions made by people for people because what people really want is to forget that, somewhere inside, their hungry skeletons are reaching out for the something behind the wall of distraction.

For many millennia now, the primitive (and then slightly less primitive) human being has peered into the canopy of space overhead, an upright ape reaching into it with a soul full of longing, wanting so bad for something behind and beyond all this. In the ancients' blood-soaked foolishness, they sacrificed children to curry the approval and favor of whatever divine power looked down into the dome of human darkness—approval and favor that can never be conjured by behaviors or bloodletting; approval that was already theirs long before they steadied the blade over the trembling child. Human beings wrote and read and studied rule books, practically killing themselves to uphold each line item with exact specificity, killing others who refused to acknowledge those same rules, beholden to other powers and gods. They starved themselves, set themselves on fire—anything and everything to send a message into the mysterious heavens: *Do you see me? Will you know me? I was here. I mattered. I didn't want to be alone.*

But they weren't alone. They never were. The terrible irony of the great command at the heart of this book is that the decree requires not initiative but reciprocation. We love because we were loved first. But why? What in sad, scrambling humanity—primitive, then slightly less so—did the omnipotent God over all creation deem so fundamentally loveable that he would willfully give himself for humanity's sake? Just you—with all your secret garbage, your terrible inconsistencies, the tangle of contradictions that is you. The God who is, fundamentally, love could do no other but act in eternal accordance with love. He loved us first. He loves us now.

And God broke down the walls erected by primitive (and then slightly less primitive) man in order to come near to us. He made himself known to us in story and song, in parable and poem, in practice and prayer, in presence and power. But even these sacred things we domesticate. Even these ancient and holy gifts we gut, unburdening them of their mystery and mysticism, like a carcass readied for taxidermy. We make God practical and palatable. We make him a country club, a spiritual chore, a social agreement, a partisan political position, a bumper sticker. Belief becomes intellectual assent ("I think in my head something is true") rather than a sacred bond of mind, body, and soul ("I embody with my lifestyle that which is true"). The religious imagination shrivels, gasps for air, and dies. A beached whale. A skeleton in a cave.

But the love of God is a powerful, devastating force that, like a tsunami, changes all it touches. Love saturates the dried husk of the religious imagination, and it reconfigures, spongelike, growing. The love of God refuses to be chained by the narrow paradigms of the bankrupt soul, refuses to honor narrow, man-made economies of justice, is oblivious to desperate redefinition. The love of God will not flow through channels of tribalism or political power, will not be contained by our little parades and dances. God's love is not a weekend retreat, not a self-help program or a fitness regimen. The primitive (and then slightly less primitive) human stands before the encroaching tidal wave of God's love, shouting into its monolithic grandeur, demanding that it reshape itself, that it calm itself, to wait patiently until granted passage. "These are our terms!" we shout up at the towering wall of ocean. "Now, adhere to these conditions, and we will allow this wave to break." But it will not adhere. It waits for nothing. It crashes and floods. What it touches, it changes. Again and again, it changes us. All of living is a series of deaths.

When I was a boy, I looked at discarded cicada shells with disgust. They clung by the dozens to bicycle tires, tree bark, and Spanish moss, stiff and sad-looking, as frail as eggshells. They'd appear during the terrible Georgia summer, an ominous promise that insects of mammoth proportions were somewhere nearby, just out of sight. You could hear them chittering in the foliage, the constant white noise of the outdoors. When I was a boy, my friends and I wrongly referred to them as locust shells, not knowing the last of the North American locusts died out more than a hundred years prior. That boy explored rural southern forests and creek beds. He used a stick to sweep empty exoskeletons from leaves and tree stumps. He heard the terrible thrumming chorus of a hundred cicadas somewhere in the brush, a distant drone, proof of the incredible accomplishment of the metamorphosis; but that boy rarely saw the changed cicadas, freed from the prison of their previous selves.

One of the only cicadas I laid eyes on before leaving the South was held captive in an empty plastic soda bottle. Another kid had somehow captured it before it molted, and it emerged to find itself taken hostage. A few of us gathered around the bottle where it crawled on twigs and brown detritus, drubbing its great wings against the inside of the bottle, eyes like dull rubies on either side of its black head, a tiny hammerhead shark. The discarded shell rattled lifelessly in the bottle.

"It doesn't look anything like it used to," someone said. All of us mumbled our agreement.

All of living is a series of deaths. You are always emerging from one and on the precipice of another. This book is the next precipice.

BOOK ONE: RUINER

PARABLE

I. FIRST, THE ENTIRE
STORY IN SUMMATION

II.–III. THEN, THREE
DISTINCT BUT RELATED
STORIES IMPORTANT
FOR UNDERSTANDING
THE WHOLE

IV. A BRIEF HISTORY OF
THE MOVEMENT SO FAR

V.–VI. FINALLY, SOME
THINGS CHRISTIANS
BELIEVE AS A RESULT

ANOTHER PARABLE

"I was born in a puddle of
blood wanting everything.
The blood was my own, pumping
through my infant heart.
I weighed myself and found myself
wanting, wanting everything.
Wanting everything is the thing that
eventually tears you apart."

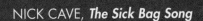

NICK CAVE, *The Sick Bag Song*

"None of us will escape death—the most radical manifestation of brokenness."

HENRI NOUWEN, *Life of the Beloved*

PARABLE: THE SINFUL PARISHIONER

I LIKE GETTING TO church early, before anyone else. I like the way the wood groans beneath my feet and peals throughout the sanctuary. I like how the pew pops and creaks when I sit. I like the crisp, starchy crackle of paper as I open my Bible and turn its pages. I come here early to pray.

I sit in the front and face the pulpit, and I give thanks. *Thank you, God, for my life. Thank you for the wisdom and discipline necessary to be here at all, to come early, before everyone else, and to pray. How many foolish decisions could I have made but did not, God? My life might be in shambles had I sinned, like so many others. But I did not. Thank you. I am grateful, God, that my gaze is not lecherous. That I have earned all that is rightfully mine. That my hands have known no bloodshed. There are so many lost souls,*

God. The streets are crowded with them. More than there've ever been. Thank you that I am not among them.

All week, protestors had clogged the sidewalks—reprobates insisting on evil laws and lawmakers, forever warring with godly governments and leaders. They would shout at my car as I passed, seeing my bumper stickers and hating them, hating me for putting them there. I'd lock eyes with them, moving as if in slow motion, grieved by their foolishness and evil. *Your time is coming*, I'd think. *Soon. Thank God*, I'd pray. *Thank God I am not among them.*

One morning, as I was praying these things, my concentration was broken by the sanctuary door. It yawned open with a noisy whine, and there stood a quavering vagrant, stinking of his lifestyle and bad decisions. I was humbled by the sight of him, by the power of my sound living. *Thank God it isn't me*, I thought. Our eyes connected, and I recognized him, the same sneering face I'd seen behind his protest sign, snarling his venom as I watched him pass from my car window.

The wicked man took no note of me. He showed no respect for the sacredness of the sanctuary itself but fell where he stood at the entrance and wept, as undignified in the presence of God as he was on the street corner. His cabled neck ratcheting downward, unable or unwilling to look to heaven, he barked his noisy, clamoring prayer into the floorboards.

"Oh God," he mewled. "Oh my God. I need you. I need you. Please. Please look at me. Please help me. I'm broken, God. I'm undone. Now I'm nothing. Oh God, please help me."

He carried on like this until the awful racket made it almost impossible to pray. Really pray, I mean.

I. A SHORT NOTE ON THE HISTORY OF LIFE AND DEATH

NOW THE LAND WAS wild and waste—an abyssal plain of useless, chaotic nonexistence. But Yahweh was there—had been there. God the Father, God the Son, God the Holy Spirit, already pouring themselves out in love. And the creative love of God overflowed. The Spirit of God hovered over the chaos. The Father spoke, and through his Word, the artistry of God took shape.

God made the sky and the land. He inaugurated and ordered time itself, as the light of his glory carved a great dichotomy between night and day and set the eternal clicking mechanisms of time in place, somewhere within the whirring heart of the universe he designed. And God split the chaotic ocean of nothingness in two, and he called up dry ground from within the waters. He summoned from its crags and valleys coiling ivy and towering cedars. He conjured from their branches glistening fruit and florid blossoms.

God drew his finger to the heavens and set in them spiraling galaxies, luminous nebulas, and blazing icons of fiery light. God fixed them with the rhythm of the universe and dressed them to reflect his heavenly glory as visual symbols of an invisible truth painted in the velvet black dome of sky. God created and appointed spiritual beings in the divine realm to worship him and serve his purposes.

And God set feathered birds and leathery-winged reptiles in the sky. They went soaring over a horizon as new as wet paint. He reached into the midnight zone of the sea and populated it with undulating mollusks and phosphorescent anglerfish, their mouths crowded with translucent fangs.

And on the land, he designed aardvarks and crocodiles. God, the first and best artist, drew for himself blue cassowary birds and orange fruit bats. All of it—the time cogs of the universe, the night and the day, the valleys and tundra, the ferns and eucalyptus and pomegranates, the archaeopteryx and the sparrow, the colossal squid, the clownfish, the monitor lizards, and polar bears—all of it was good. But then God, the first and best artist, leaned forward. With deft precision, he drew the symphony of his creative masterwork to crescendo and set in the garden wilderness human beings; up from the dirt, naked, their pink lungs inflating with their first gulps of raw oxygen. Set in the wild garden of his artistry, God designed humanity in his own image. In the image of God, he created them. Male and female, he created them. He set them in a garden of his own creation—all of it was his own creation.

And it was very good.

And so, the story begins in a garden home. The crisp dew of a morning that has not yet known discord or decay. All of life flourishing. The graceful antelope leap by unpolluted rivers as clear as shimmering glass. They drink their fill and nestle beside the feral lion. Together, they share a meal of figs in the warm grass and are satisfied. Over the scene: the great and glorious artist. The Father, the Son, and the Spirit. He who moves his mighty hands like a maestro's baton and, from his imagination, spins spiraling galaxies and spools out stars ablaze like lanterns in the darkness of space. Flowering plants and thrumming insects, lumbering mastodons and swimming serpents like reptilian ribbons in a bright blue sea.

But the artist is more than creator. He is the origin and source of the most powerful force in all the universe—the creator, God, *is* love. From the overflowing lavishness of his great love, God crafts for himself company. Men and women. Kings and queens, made to rule and reign over the wild, good world. Trusting God, trusting his decree of goodness, they are to fill and subdue creation. God does not see fit to rule from the intimidating tower of an inaccessible throne. He steps down, his feet warm in the grass, arm in arm with his kings and his queens, and with excitement, he commissions them: "Join me! Trust me. Make something out of all this! Something good!"

The sacred human beings—who bear God's image—are to act as God's reflection and representatives in God's created order. God appoints them to oversee all he has made and to exercise his loving dominion over sunflowers and oceans and rainforests, and over one another. God is the family who makes more family, and he invites the human beings to reach out and seize the open hand of their Creator God, as his partners and collaborators, to do good in and to his world.

Or not. They don't have to. They get to choose. To allow for no choice would be tyranny, not love. So, "Choose," God says. Choose to draw life and love from God and to define goodness from the wellspring of God's eternal, relational reign. Or choose to define life and love and goodness all on your own—on the infantile "wisdom" that climbs up from the dirt at the command of God. God invites: "Trust me. I love you." But a voice whispers into the dark corners of the human heart: "God is a liar."

A flash of fangs. A flickering forked tongue. *God is a liar.* An infiltrator in God's good garden. The adversary. Once heavenly servant to the purposes of God, in eons past, the adversary challenged God's throne—a created thing desperate to supplant its creator. It hurtled like a meteor into God's world, penetrating the earth, a terrible crater out of which crawled sadness and sickness and death—all the things that stand in mockery and defiance of who God is and what God does. The adversary—a murderer from the beginning, red in tooth and claw. It slithered into God's garden armed with a lie. And given the choice of abundant life with God, as it was in the beginning, or the squalor and death of their own dominion on their own terms, humanity opts for new management, and everything breaks and dies and rots.

And with the wallpaper of creation blackened and peeling, with millennia of violence and depravity on the horizon—the inevitable horrors of a world bent toward defiance against the God of love—God yet makes a promise: "I won't let things end this way. I'll send someone." He promises the fallen kings and queens that in the distant reaches of their genealogy someone will come. A better king. This new and better king will succeed where they failed. He will go to war against the adversary and crush the liar who has led the humans astray, though the battle will find the serpent's fangs buried in the king's heel. This victory will come at a terrible cost.

God's promise reverberates over the crumbling goodness of the garden: "This will not be the end of the story." Black toxins cloud the once glass-like river, the lion tears the flesh of the antelope, wasps fill the fig, and it falls and decays in the soil. Where once the vocation of humans was charged with the electricity of creative energy, work becomes complicated with struggle and pain. Where once work was joy, it is now dried by joylessness. The humans will perpetually go about clawing at one another for rank and power and position, convinced of their own wisdom apart from God.

Enmity grew like briars between humans—and their potential collided with an ending, and the ending was called death. The idyllic peacefulness of the garden was usurped by violence and tragedy, hatefulness and corruption. And in the end, they died. And as the lion wets his lips with the blood of the antelope, so we, humanity, wet our lips with the blood of our brothers and sisters and with the blood of creation itself.

And the world entered its long winter, a downward spiral into chaos—violence, murder, betrayal, the scrambling for status and trampling one another. And in the story, we, these fallen kings and queens, lament, fists raised to a seemingly indifferent sky: God, why won't you do something about this awful mess?

God might have wiped the slate of this failed experiment clean. He might have answered our pleas to eradicate evil by eradicating us. But the artist is more than creator. He is love. So, God makes good on his promise. God initiates a rescue plan.

He again beckons to his human collaborators—"Come, let us put together these broken pieces. I am not yet prepared to abandon this dream of mine." But the barbed tendrils of evil have so burrowed themselves in the heart of humanity that to uproot evil would mean destroying that which God loves so dearly: us. His fallen kings and his fallen queens.

Because, like visitors in God's museum, we have beheld God's masterpiece for only moments before we set to work tearing it apart with our bare hands, hurling upon it buckets of black ink, dousing it with our spit, defiling it with excrement. All of us. With contributions great and small, we all participate in the vandalism of God's desired good for us, for the world. In our clamoring up the backs of others to do ourselves good, we have brought our appointed rule to staggering disrepair. And through it all, God opts to love us anyway. And the ticking cogs of the universe click clockwise. Time marches on.

On a day in human history, God spoke to people again—as he had done before, as he had done in the beginning—and he made with them a covenant. A promise. Marriage vows: "I will love you. I will begin my rescue mission in you. The snake—the adversary—will be crushed, and I will rescue the world." Beholden to a broken humanity, God chooses one from the many—a man called Abram—and God tells Abram the king is still coming. He will rise up from the long bloodline of Abram's descendants. God gives Abram the name Abraham— the father of many—and Abraham's family blossoms into the tribe of Israel, and God extends his covenant promise over Israel, inviting them to become his collaborative partners once again—unique in all the world—through whom God will restore the goodness of the garden. And again, God promises, the king is still coming.

Another morning.

The crisp dew of a sunrise that has known discord and decay and knows them well. All of life feeding off of and destroying itself in the cycle of sin and death. A priest of Israel steps before an altar and, with a heavy heart, begins the sacrifice. In it, a blameless animal—a frightened lamb—will be slaughtered as a powerful symbol, a reminder of the great cost of evil, the toll it takes, the debt it creates, that evil always summons death, and that death always heeds its summons. Somehow, in this profound and symbolic gesture, the guilt of humanity—the vandalism of God's goodness—will be transferred to the shivering animal. Its blood will pour out. A sobering visual of its very life draining away, and Israel remembers that evil is costly, the fracturing of relationship destructive, the power of death unforgiving.

This priest will wander the Temple with guilt-laden spirit, sprinkling the animal's blood as a symbol of life washing away the horrible consequences of evil. And yet, the cycle carries on until Israel no longer brings their sacrificial lambs with heavy hearts, but as empty ritual. A ceremonial chore. The obligation of blood with no pain of cost, empty religious pageantry, as beyond the Temple walls depravity and discord unspool from the hearts of those created to do good in God's world, but who can manage only evil. And God pleads with his people from the mouths of prophets: "Remember the covenant! The marriage vows!"

But Israel will not listen.

Among Israel's kings, no promised savior can be found—only bloodthirsty warlords, lecherous abusers, swindlers, rapists, and megalomaniacs. The snake always hangs about their shoulders, a foul necklace, whispering, *God is a liar*. And the evils of Israel compound until the nation itself topples under the weight of its own corruption and injustice. Foreign invaders plunder the land, destroy the Temple, and take God's people away into exile.

Into the darkness of Israel's sin, a prophet called Isaiah speaks again of something yet to happen: the long-foretold, snake-crushing king—just as God promised in the disintegrating garden. "He will," Isaiah says, "deal with evil once and for all. But hear this. This king is not who we expect him to be. This promised king will become a servant. He will suffer, and he will die." And Isaiah's words fall on deaf ears.

God warned and pleaded and reminded his people of their call to be kings and queens, to do good, but they would not listen. In the face of compounding evil, God—his heart heavy with grief at their unfaithfulness—allows Israel to be overtaken and destroyed. Driven from their homes. No land. No king. No Temple. Everything breaking and broken.

And the whirring day-to-night-and-back-again clock of the universe ticks on. Then: another morning. The crisp dew of a sunrise that knows discord and decay and knows them well. All of life feeding off of and destroying itself in the cycle of sin and death. In a nowhere corner of an empire forged from the rubble of fallen Israel. In a nothing village. In a nobody household. God speaks to a poor teenage girl.

Through a messenger, God tells this young woman, "The king is finally coming. The suffering servant. The one who will confront and deal with evil. The one who will rescue. You," he tells the girl, "will be his mother." The same Spirit who hovered over the chaotic waters in creation hovered over Mary and conceived new creation in her womb, though she was a virgin.

The king's name will be Yeshua—Jesus. His name means "Yahweh rescues." But he's also called *Emmanuel*, which means "God with us." This king, this *God with us*, does not arrive in a chariot of fire, or as a sword-wielding warrior, or as an intangible cosmic force descending a heavenly staircase. He arrives as a human baby born to poor teenagers in a cave. He comes to us in the darkness. In our darkness. The king comes to us not protected by an impenetrable divine aura but blood-streaked and screaming, as babies do, soundtracked by his mother's cries of pain and struggle, of lowing cows and bleating goats. He arrives in the nauseating copper tinge of blood and the heavy, fetid stink of waste. The Word in and through whom all things were created, who was present with the Father as the Spirit hovered over the waters when the land was wild and waste, descends from heaven and from the birth canal of his human mother, as she strains and cries, an eruption of fluids and prayers. Overlooked and ignored by religious and political power, the Word is swaddled in the darkness as buzzing flies encircle livestock and afterbirth.

And by angels, God calls forth not chief priests nor emperors to behold the newborn king, but poor shepherds. I have good news for worthless people! God's reign and redemption are coming to invert power and oppression and to proclaim hope to the poor.

The king grows in poverty and obscurity. He learns. And finally, when the time is right, he initiates his rescue mission proper. The mission to eradicate evil, to bring about mercy and goodness for all of humanity, for all the cosmos. He wanders ancient Israel with dust-covered feet that bring the seditious good news of a new king and a new kingdom. And as the prophets once promised throughout the Hebrew Scriptures, Jesus heals the sick, brings good news to the poor, works in the ways of justice and compassion—and in this strange and unexpected way, a splintering fissure appears in the way things are. A crack, nearly imperceptible but spreading. And through it shines a light. Because this king, this long-promised, long-awaited rescuer of Israel, is more than a man. He speaks with authority. He walks upon the waves of the sea. He forgives sins. He is I AM—God come to us in flesh and blood. God with us.

But the old story repeats itself.

On a serpentine tongue come the questions, then accusations. *Must God be in charge? Is he truly good? Ought we not rule ourselves? God is lying. He isn't good. We can do better.* And Jesus, this rescuing king, is shackled and dragged into the darkness of an evil night. He is scourged, beaten, mocked. They hit him, profane him, spit on him. And those who had loved and followed him watch as the dream falls apart, and they abandon him to the darkness. This would-be king is brought to humiliating ruin. Naked, nailed to a cross—the most agonizing instrument of torture and execution the Roman Empire has to offer. He was to be king, but now he dies like the worst of common criminals. Stripped naked and bleeding before his mother and his friends, accursed, the snake's fangs fastened to his heel just as God said they would be.

He was to be great and mighty, but here he hangs, wheezing, seized by bodily tremors, barely maintaining consciousness. There will be no kingdom, and there will be no king. And as the lion wets his lips with the blood of the antelope, so we, humanity, wet our lips with the blood of our brothers and sisters, with the blood of creation, and with the blood of this would-be king: God with us. His body split open; the blood of life runs out as it did from the slaughtered lamb on the altar. A reminder of the great cost of evil, the toll it takes, the debt it creates. Evil always summons death, and death always heeds its summons.

The ancient Scriptures make the incredible claim that, somehow, in this moment, the guilt of humanity—the vandalism of God's goodness—would be transferred to this shivering sacrificial lamb. His blood pours out, and he remembers evil is costly, the fracturing of relationship destructive, the power of death unforgiving. His tattered body lies cold and lifeless, wrapped in the linen of the grave and tucked in the darkness of a tomb. There will be no kingdom, and there will be no king. All is lost.

Until ...

In the darkness of the tomb, when all hope is lost, beneath the grave linens, God begins to mend the broken body of Jesus.

A heart, still for days, trembles in his chest.

Then beats.

Then beats again.

A warmth begins to spread through what was, moments prior, a corpse.

God undoing death.

Terrified, the old snake, the one who leads the entire world astray, tightens his desperate grip of death around Jesus and finds he can hold it no longer.

The once-unbreakable chains of mortality melt away like wax before a flame, and though all the evil of history had crushed him unto death, Jesus sits up, and the evil falls away, a withering wisp of ash disappearing in the air around him. A stone had been set before the tomb to keep grave robbers out, but the stone cannot keep the risen Jesus in. And as Jesus crosses the threshold of a grave he was meant to inhabit until his lifeless body was dust, a skeleton, a locust's shell, the old curse is broken forever. The king is alive. The kingdom has come.

Beholden to his risen glory and forever changed, the king's apprentices begin to carry the beautiful, subversive movement of Jesus to the ends of the earth. That the King of Kings, the Prince of Peace, the God of love and justice and goodness has come to rescue humanity in a poor peasant rabbi, executed as an enemy of the state. They write his teachings on their hearts, stumbling and imperfect though they are, and give themselves over in discipleship to the master so that the ways of justice and peace blossom from a tiny, grassroots subculture into a movement sweeping out across the globe—the church. And when the skeptics cry treachery, when the religious cry blasphemy, they can only point to the empty tomb. "Look! He has risen just like he said."

With nothing to gain and everything to lose, they live and die on this claim so that it becomes a sword twisting through the split skull of the beaten serpent. And centuries later, historians puzzle over ancient biographies and wonder, How could it be so? Why would the first Christians face poverty and persecution and death on a claim that, if it were not true, they, of all people, would have known it wasn't? Why, unless they believed it to be true? Was it a trick? A hallucination? A kind of contagious madness?

But his apprentices only point to the tomb. "It's empty. Look! Just like he said."

The long-promised kingdom was inaugurated by the king on the promise of resurrection. The resilient battle cry: "What God did for Jesus, he will do for all of humanity and for creation itself." Not an afterlife. The "afterlife" was as common a belief in the ancient world as in the modern. Resurrection is different. "Afterlife" is the idea that there is *something else* after and beyond this awful mess—an ellipsis fastened to the final statement of death. Yes, we die, but ... *then* we'll go elsewhere. That is not the story of the resurrection.

Resurrection is not an ellipsis but a confrontational no to the final statement of death. "No. Death will not have the final word. God is not done with me, not done with the body he knit together in my mother's womb, not done with a world he made good, not done with plants and animals and families and art and culture." Evil always summons death, and death always heeds its summons, but resurrection makes fools of them both. The snake is as good as dead.

This broken, hurting world will not end in ruin nor the darkness of death but in the triumph of resurrection, and us with it. I shall rise again. The grave, only temporary. What the Father God has done for his son, Jesus, he will do for the entire cosmos. And on a coming day, Jesus will usher in the renewal of all things. He will gather up the molecules of every dead and decomposed body, of every pile of ashes. He will reach into tombs and caves to collect the dust of ancient skeletons, and he will reform and renew our bodies—joining with them the immaterial part of us that has waited with God in the sleep of death. And King Jesus will do the same act of cosmic revival to all of creation. God will repair, not abandon, his good world.

Imperfect and broken though they have been in the slow churn of the first age, any man and any woman may accept the free gift of the creative outpouring of love that spoke the universe into existence, raised Jesus from the dead, and will renew all things. Having no way to earn his great love—they can accept it freely given and enter into the eternal loving union of the everlasting kingdom. The world made new and us in it. And to those who even still will not bend before God's loving goodness, God will honor their decision freely made and hand them over to the everlasting destruction they prefer. This parade of darkness and despair is coming to an end; we know this because of King Jesus, and we will defy the snake until the king destroys him once and for all. Where now our world is marred by animosity and discord, by sin, suffering, despair, and death, the resurrection of Jesus—a single moment in human history—is the promise these things will come to an end.

And it is very good.

THE APOSTLES' CREED

I believe in God, the Father almighty,

creator of heaven and earth.

I believe in Jesus Christ, his only Son, our Lord,

who was conceived by the Holy Spirit

and born of the virgin Mary.

He suffered under Pontius Pilate,

was crucified, died, and was buried;

he descended to hell.

The third day he rose again from the dead.

He ascended to heaven

and is seated at the right hand of God the
Father almighty.

From there he will come to judge the living
and the dead.

I believe in the Holy Spirit,

the holy universal church,

the communion of saints,

the forgiveness of sins,

the resurrection of the body,

and the life everlasting. Amen.

THOUSANDS OF YEARS AGO—MAYBE AROUND
THE THIRTEENTH CENTURY BC—NEAR THE
BEGINNING OF OUR STORY.

II. THE DESTROYER

A YOUNG ISRAELITE WOMAN gnashes her teeth in the throes of labor pain. This is not the world into which a new mother hopes to deliver her first child. The stories the others have been telling bear down on her as she herself bears down. Those stories. Living nightmares. But long before screaming and weeping found her village, there had been happiness, even among slaves—the only life she'd ever known. Like her mother before her and her mother before her.

She'd been married, then her belly swelled, and there had been celebration—tears of joy rather than agony. A reprieve in the slave's world of hurt. But today, the rumors of these terrible times hang like darkness in the air as Hebrew midwives gather around her, and she pushes, and she hears for the first time the tiny trembling cry of her newborn son. The baby is lifted to her arms, naked and sobbing, and her tears mingle with his, and she is swept up in the kind of euphoric love only mothers know.

She cradles the tiny boy at her breast and nurses him, and for long moments, it seems as if she might drown in love—a love so profound, localized in a space so small, tucked in the crook of her arm, pressed to the warmth of her chest.

Until she hears them coming.

The Egyptians. Drawn to the news of the baby like flies to death, they come. The blood thrums in her head, the panic rises in her throat, and she calls to her husband. The midwives rush to lead the men away, but the baby cries out, and in an instant, the Egyptians are upon her. Weak though she is, she resists, her midwives pleading, her husband fighting back. But they take the boy, snatching his tiny, fragile body from arms meant to protect him. Arms that fail him now.

She gives chase until she collapses. The sound of her son screeching is eclipsed by the hammering of horse hooves as the Egyptians disappear. It is the last she'll ever hear his voice. She weeps and bleeds in the dust.

And the decree of the Egyptian king echoes in the faculties of her skull: "Every Hebrew boy that is born you must throw into the Nile." As if spoken by a dark voice into her broken heart, she hears it again and again and again. And neither sleep nor peace can find her beneath the impenetrable dome of her sorrow. She thinks of the boy every moment of every day. But the cruelty of time's indifference carries her on, brokenhearted, into the next day and the next. A terrible blackness swallows everything.

A year passes, and she conceives again, but just beneath the first flutter of joy comes the all-encompassing dread. Her husband holds her at night as she shivers and sobs, clinging to her belly as if she can protect the baby from the evil beyond the womb. She reasons with her husband that they might flee, but how? Aren't they prisoners in this land? Just slaves? If the Egyptians don't kill them, the desert will. So, for nine months, she prays. Until the day comes.

She cries out to God, as she did for nine long months, for a girl. The Egyptians will spare a girl. Please, God, a girl. But as the midwives call for a final push, and as the baby emerges, she sees the looks on the midwives' faces—the way they twist—and she knows. She holds the little boy and cries. "Please, God. Not again. Not again."

So, she hides the boy and, with her husband, plans their escape—but the Egyptians come once again, and when they take the boy, she wants to go with him into the waters and, like him, breathe no more. The waters, she has been told since she was a little girl, are chaos and evil. She thinks about the waters of the Nile closing over her head—and the Nile might as well be the sea. She thinks about sinking. About how cold it would be. How dark. And then maybe it would stop hurting. Then maybe she could hold her sons again.

But they take the baby and leave the mother, as they did so many times before. Countless boys stripped from countless begging mothers before her and after her.

Another day comes, oblivious to her broken heart. And another. And water becomes for her a harbinger of death. Even floating in clay pots, it mocks her, like rippling pools of evil itself. Years go by. And the pain of her missing sons gives way to the pain of never finding herself pregnant again, even when she and her husband are bold enough to try.

So, her heart becomes barren and can produce no more prayers. She, like her mother before her, knows suffering under Egyptian whips and cruelty under Egyptian slavers. And, as with her mother before her, tears and dust are her food day and night. As the terrible years ebb like sand on stone, she watches as so many friends and cousins and aunts and uncles, her own mother and father, collapse, or are beaten to death, or are dragged away for punishment, never to return. She often wishes it was over, but the years mock her until all hope has long dried, and where once she carried sadness and despair, she eventually carries only numbness and antipathy. The sea—the waters of chaos and evil—surge over her world in every way.

She is much older when the man comes.

A stranger from the East, in Midian. A man of her people, but she does not know him. He gathers their elders together and says, "Yahweh, the God of your fathers—the God of Abraham, Isaac, and Jacob—appeared to me and said, 'I have watched over you and have seen what has been done to you in Egypt.' Yahweh is concerned about you and has seen your misery, and he will bring you out of slavery in Egypt."

When word of his announcement reaches her, she scowls, the skin gathering across her wrinkled forehead and face, and she feels the familiar sting of tears in the corners of her tired eyes. The audacity of this stranger. Now? When she is an old woman? Now God "sees" what has been done? He's "concerned"? Where before her tired heart felt almost nothing, she now feels a seething animosity toward this stranger and toward God. As if to punctuate her acrimony, things get worse because of the stranger, not better. He marches into Pharaoh's throne room, as if he is anything other than no one, and demands the release of her people. The king of Egypt is so insulted by the stranger's foolish daring that he forces her people to gather the straw that was once supplied to them, doubling their labor. And when her people collapse in exhaustion, they are beaten to the brink of death. Her heart further darkens against the stranger and God.

Until the day someone tells her about the Nile. She hears the others murmuring about it—the dead fish, the terrible coppery stink, the undrinkable water, the corrupted earth, no longer fertile. The Nile—a river she kept closed off from her wandering mind—has become blood. *God* turned the Nile to blood—as if he is declaring judgment on Egypt; as if he is saying, "I know what you did." But for the woman, it is too little and too late.

Then all the water in Egypt—the streams and canals, even the water in jars—all turns, as it had in her mind so many years ago, to blood. Then, up from the blood bubbles frogs—legions of them. Enough to blanket the roads and festoon the Egyptian doorways. Enough to infest Egyptian homes. Throngs of them, wet skin glistening, green and mottled brown, thousands of shining black eyes in Egyptian palaces and beds and food stores. She watches in disbelief as the world itself becomes an undulating tapestry of frogs.

She asks the others what is happening. *Was the blood not enough?* Her heart goes cold at their answer. The Lord is pleading with Pharaoh. God is giving the Egyptians opportunities to repent.

Then come buzzing gnats and swarming flies. Then, the animals of Egypt keel over and rot in the field. The stench of carcasses is conjoined to the stink of festering boils as Egyptian skin swells red and dribbles foul-smelling pus. Her heart races for the first time in years as she sees the horrors of a world unraveling, just as the stranger said it would. As God said it would. The stranger comes again to her village and urges them all inside. A terrible hailstorm is coming. She watches as the sky casts down great thudding hunks of ice and flashing bolts of lightning in the distance over Egypt but stands baffled as not a fleck reaches the land where her people wait. Her old eyes squint through the gale at the homes of the Egyptians in the distance, and she calculates their cruelty and foolishness. She almost asks God why he does not simply crush them, but this is too much like a prayer, so she says nothing at all.

The locusts come next, covering the world as the frogs had until it becomes a writhing mass of insect legs, a chittering legion, destroying all that was left after the hail. The land itself becomes as hollow as a molted exoskeleton. The air hums with them—a deafening drone like an invasion of soldiers descending on the scattered remnants of Egypt. And when the corruption of their life's water, the infestation of grotesqueries and bane against their livestock could not stir the Egyptians to repentance, when neither yawning sores in their putrid flesh, nor thundering boulders of ice, nor even an army of devouring locusts could sway them, darkness envelops Egypt. A darkness so solid as to be completely impenetrable, day and night, for three long, disorienting days. And finally, the stranger appears again. "The cavalcade of divine horror and wonder will now crescendo," he says. "The firstborn of Egypt are going to die."

The Israelite woman's blood curdles in her veins. Where were *her* nine routes of escape? Why was she given no means of escape when those who do evil have been given many? The stranger lays out his peculiar instructions, given by God himself, and she joins her people in the first Passover. She watches, a strange ache in her chest, as they slaughter the lamb and smear its blood across the doorframes. God will see the blood, the stranger said, and he will not permit the Destroyer to enter their houses or to strike their firstborn down.

After nine miracles, God is still providing a way out.

Long after the events of that dark night of the Destroyer, when a Hebrew author puts sacred pen to sacred papyrus, inspired by the Spirit of God himself to tell this sacred story, with no word left to chance, the author writes, "The blood will be a sign for you on the houses where you are, and when I see the blood, I will protect you. I will defend you." A promise that God would not allow the Destroyer into their homes. The Destroyer. The adversary. The snake.

The Israelite woman has been taught from childhood that dark and terrible forces of chaos surround God's ordered goodness of creation—like an oasis with desert on all sides—and that there are times when created things so persist in their unwillingness to receive God's good and gracious reign over that oasis that God grieves and relaxes his protection, so that agents of chaos and de-creation can needle the bubble of our otherwise ordered world—and those so insistent on evil are given what they badly want: life without God. (Put another way, death.)

After centuries of patience, and after nine explicit warnings and miraculous sign-acts and pleas for repentance, Yahweh loosens his grip on order, and the Destroyer enters the homes of Egypt to steal, kill, and destroy. And even then, not without restraint. Yahweh will protect every house sheltered by the blood of the lamb—be it Hebrew or Egyptian. "But the time has come. I will bring judgment," Yahweh announces, "on all the gods of Egypt." For Yahweh is not allowing chaos to overwhelm and destroy mere human systems of evil and oppression, but the spiritual systems of evil that animate them. And the Destroyer goes through Egypt with such devastation that Pharaoh, if only for a moment, yields. The king of Egypt releases the Israelites from their slavery just as God and the stranger said he would.

The Israelite woman follows behind the stranger, the man called Moses, as they wander into a land and a future both unknown, and she puzzles within herself as they go. She is still angry. Angry that God did not rescue her children. Angry he did not deliver her or her people all those long years before. And angry at his patience with Egypt. She is angry that he included them in his mercy, that he provided them warnings and protection from the Destroyer should they only receive both as free gifts.

Where was her protection when she needed it? Why did he not warn her when the Egyptians were coming or provide a path on which to flee? The waters—that chaos and evil—had long been over her head; all her life they were drowning her. And as she wanders with her people—and freed, liberated Israel arrives at the Red Sea—she remembers her suffering; not that she had ever forgotten it. And she hears the thundering drone of Pharaoh's chariots. Hordes of his troops barreling through the dunes toward helpless Israel. Her people shout, "Was it because there were no graves in Egypt that you brought us to the desert to die? What have you done to us by bringing us out of Egypt?"

They say to the stranger, to Moses, "Didn't we say to you in Egypt, 'Leave us alone; let us serve the Egyptians'? It would have been better for us to serve the Egyptians than to die in the desert!"

And with the evil she has known all her life—Egypt and the sea—both behind and before her, she closes her eyes and listens as the hammering of hooves synchronizes with the drumming of her old heart against her rib cage. She breathes deeply of sand and dust, and she thinks, *Perhaps all my sorrows end here in pitiful tragedy.* She shivers when she feels the spray of water on her face and opens her eyes to behold the sea itself split in half before her eyes—helpless against the terrible majesty of God.

Between the great walls of obedient water lies the dry ground—and her people are passing through the water, out of chaos and oppression into something else. So, she rises and walks. She sees then that while God did not engineer her suffering, he did design her redemption—glorious to behold. As she passes through the sea, her heart begins to thaw. An old callus warms, erodes, and falls away.

She sees a young Egyptian mother hemmed in on all sides by Israelites. A woman who accepted God's pleas and left everything she has known. The Egyptian woman holds a baby boy to her chest as she passes through the broken sea. And the Israelite woman feels the familiar sting of tears in the corners of her tired eyes—tears not of pure sorrow nor pure joy, but something else. For the first time in a long time, the Israelite woman smiles and begins to pray.

The story was told and told again. It was written and read for hundreds of years, a thousand and more, so that every Israelite child would know each of its twists and turns by heart, just as they would reenact that Passover meal year in and year out. Israel was, all those generations later, still waiting to be rescued, not from an Egyptian slave driver, but from the adversary, the snake, the Destroyer.

The Passover acknowledged generations of pain and struggle and hope and life. It brought that story of salvation and longing into the present, around a dinner table with family and friends who belonged to the same story, who were waiting with the same hope and anticipation. Until one day, a man called Yeshua Ha-Notzri (Jesus who is from Nazareth) redefined the Passover meal around himself. Born into a time when his people were oppressed, he, like Moses, escaped a genocide of baby boys. He wandered in the desert before coming to his people with news of liberation. And Jesus understood himself as the lamb whose blood would be provided as protection against the Destroyer during a time when chaos had been loosed in the night. In Jesus, God continued his battle against both human and spiritual systems of evil—on earth and in the spiritual realm.

When God is at long last revealed not as a distant puppet master who engineers plagues in a theater of arbitrary cruelty, but as the God who comes low to creation itself and allows himself to fall before death and the Destroyer in our place, the great ocean of your pain and tragedy—past, present, and yet to come—will one day be rent like a thin curtain—and the blood of God himself, poured out in self-sacrificial love, will be the dry ground on which you pass as you follow Jesus through the split sea.

Exodus is only the second scroll in a very long redemption story. And we're still in it. But God has already demonstrated the epic of his love in his son, Jesus, the Passover lamb who takes away the sin of the world. The chaos and evil of your own life—the things you've done and the things that have been done to you—are not an ocean too imposing for Jesus to speak and split it in half, that he might provide passage from hopelessness to redemption.

THOUSANDS OF YEARS AGO—
MAYBE BEFORE 1050 BC—IN THE
EARLIER SCENES OF OUR STORY.

III. WHEN TRAGEDY FOUND THE OLD WOMAN

IT HAD BEEN NEARLY a lifetime when tragedy found the old woman—when her life became wild and waste. Whatever beacon calls out to tragedy across and beneath the broken world, it finally chimed, and tragedy answered. First, there was no food. So, the woman followed her husband and two grown sons out of the only home they'd ever known—the home of their ancestors and stories and God—and into the land of their ancient enemies. Sometimes, as they traveled, she'd cry, thinking of home, but then she would look up and see her husband and the two strong men who had once been nursing infants at her breast, and she felt brave. *If God can grow strength from such weakness*, she thought, *he can make me strong.*

In the strange land, the land of their enemies, her sons found wives, and so their family grew before it shrank. First, her husband died. Then, one after the other, her sons followed their father into the grave. She wanted to go with them. When the old woman packed what little she had left and prepared for the journey home, her two daughters-in-law were ready to follow her, but the old woman rebuked them: "Stay here," she told them. "It's over. I'm over. Whatever divine kindness I once knew has dried up, and God's tender touch has become violent. Life itself has become bitter in my mouth. Stay here. I have no more sons for you to marry, no fortune to share, no home, no hope, no future."

Hearing all this, one of the old woman's daughters-in-law went away, back to her own people and place and gods. But the other would not go. She held the weeping old woman and made her a promise: "I won't leave. No matter what." Together, the two returned to the old woman's home as the farmers were harvesting the first food in a long time. The old woman's daughter-in-law went to the fields and walked behind the harvesters, gathering up what fell, what was left behind, just as it was decreed in God's law, in keeping with his wisdom written on stone: "Don't take everything for yourself; leave the edges of the field, and don't pick up what you drop along the way. Leave it for those in need, for widows and the poor." She was both.

As she went behind them gathering food, a lone widow in the field, a good man saw her going behind the farmers, scraping together what fell. The good man, his eyes on the woman, asked a nearby worker, "Who is she?" The worker told the good man about the woman—how she had come from far away, how she had refused to abandon her mother-in-law, and how the two of them had returned to the old woman's home, widowed and without food.

The good man went to her. "I've heard about you," he said. "About your faithfulness and loyalty. May you have hope and a future." He gave her all the food she could carry and more. She had dinner with the good man and found herself smiling when he looked at her.

The woman returned home to her mother-in-law, talking about the good man, and the old woman lit up. "I'm related to that good man," she told her daughter-in-law. "He could rescue us." With no way to make money or ends meet in an ancient society, God's wisdom established safeguards for vulnerable widows; a surviving relative could marry into her family and save her and her family from a life of poverty, abuse, and indentured servitude. "He could be our last hope," the old woman said. "It's time to put the things of grief and mourning away. Go to him."

The woman did as her mother-in-law said. One night, when the good man had been working and eating and drinking to celebrate a successful harvest, he lay down on a pile of grain to rest. When he woke in the night, there was a shape beside him in the darkness. "Who's there?" the man asked.

The woman spoke. "It's me," she said. "When you met me, you prayed a blessing over me. For hope and a future. Now I'm asking you to see that blessing through, to be that hope and that future."

And the good man loved her. Along the long timeline—the downward spiral into evil and chaos—marked by powerful and debauched men who use power and position to abuse women, the good man honored the woman: "Your mother-in-law has another relative here. One who is, by law, first eligible to marry you and inherit all that should have belonged to your father-in-law and your husband. If he won't do it, I will."

The good man gathered the town elders, and he brought before them the one next in line to inherit the woman and her family's estate. "Will you redeem this family?" he asked. "You are next in line. If you won't do it, I will. Will you buy back all that was meant to be theirs?"

The one who was next in line considered the acquisition. "Yes," he said. "I'll take it."

"And," the good man added, "you must also marry this woman—the dead man's widow, to redeem her family."

The man who was next in line considered the burden of another mouth to feed, another responsibility to carry. "Then, no," he said. "I can't do it. The cost to me would be too great. The expense to my finances and resources and time is more than I am willing to pay for this redemption. If you're next, and if it means that much to you, you do it yourself."

"I will," the good man said.

He married the woman, and they had a son. Their mother-in-law, the old woman, held the baby in her arms, and when other women saw her and the way she looked at the baby, they said, "She loves him like her own son." And her new family, bound legally by marriage, became something more than a family bound by blood. That baby grew up and had a son of his own, and his son had a son, and that son became the king of Israel, from whom descended Jesus the Messiah, through whom all the world would be redeemed. One redemption becoming another, and another, and another.

The old woman's daughter-in-law had birthed hope for her from faithfulness, and in the end, home, family, and a future were hers; all of them bought back from suffering by love. Though she had lost her home, a garden ruined, and though her story had been run through by death, the terrible offspring of sin, and though the chaotic mechanism at the center of an indifferent universe was wound tight to tell a story set to conclude in loneliness and despair, it didn't. Love intervened.

Instead, the story was this: In the beginning, the old woman lost her home and her family and her hope. In the end, she found a new home and family and love and new life and a future more meaningful than she ever dared to hope. In the end, her redemption was bigger and more beautiful than she could have imagined when she was sad, stooped, and embittered by tragedy.

Redemption—real redemption, big and beautiful—cannot be incentivized by the calculus of profit or even practical sensibility. The old woman's story was redeemed because a redeemer wanted to redeem it, even at great personal expense. And when he did, the redemption he accomplished in self-sacrificial love did more than cover the old woman and her family; it went ahead of them, hundreds of years into the future, thousands and more, reaching backward and forward in time, a great and powerful bird with wings outstretched over every broken thing, the mere shadow of its wings calling up new life from soils long dead.

TWO THOUSAND YEARS AGO—
THE FIRST CENTURY—DURING
THE SECOND MAJOR ACT OF
OUR STORY.

IV. THE WELL OVERFLOWS

THE BOY WAS RAISED in enemy-occupied territory. It was the only world he ever knew, really. The same world we all know—broken and unfair. But his world was also a world of old stories. Stories about temples and kings, about mountains and miracles. Stories about parted seas and freed slaves. Stories about old widows and new life. He believed them as best as he knew how, though the well from which his people had once drawn hope and miracles had all but gone dry. The only water left—a puddle in the dirt—was the promised king.

In the promised king, the boy believed. For years, the boy had looked out on a world in which foreign oppressors, like Egypt before them, had seized the land from his people—these cruel Roman masters with their armor and opulence, who taxed his family into poverty, who took from them farms and livestock and homes, who cared nothing for their miracles and mountains and split seas handed down across generations, who had drained the well of hope dry.

Once, his people had laughed and married and worked and welcomed their babies and reigned in the land, enjoying the favor of their God. But his people had lost their way, forgotten their God, and became full of pride and injustice. Power cannibalizes power—a snake with its tail in its teeth, always eating. All empires fall, and so had theirs. Now, it was just a story. All of it except the king coming to set things right. The king was more than a story. The boy knew this because even the oppressor feared the coming king. Decades prior, in a terrible panic, the oppressor had slaughtered every firstborn son of his people in an effort to stop the king's coming. Do powerful men resort to such desperate ends for mere legends? No, they feared the king because the king was coming. In this, the boy believed. He had to.

He thought of the king often as he grew. He watched, helpless, as family and friends were taxed out of house and home. He saw women brutalized, children orphaned, an indifferent world that went on spinning. He imagined the king might look like him at first. *He* was not the king, he knew this, but maybe the king could come from anywhere. And anyway, who among his people was born into any power or position? No, the king would be one of them.

The boy grew up. Not having what it took to graduate from the theological schools of his people, he went with his father to work in the family trade: fish. Out on the waters, untangling nets, he'd sometimes think of the king. *To see this king,* he thought, *one of my own people*—not the military might of the oppressor, but one who would rise from poverty, his sword in his hand. He would lift the blade to the western sky, bisecting the sun, and would remind his people of the long winter of their suffering, proclaiming, "The end is nigh!" The king would lead his warriors triumphant into the heart of darkness. He would cut down the enemy presence that had grown cancerous in the land, and with the love of his people burning in his chest, the king would destroy this wickedness and take his rightful place on the throne God prepared for him as a promise to his people before he'd ever been born—the last dregs of hope in a well reduced to dust becoming an ocean that would overflow and replenish the land forever.

When the boy became a man, he would look out on the water as he fished and think of these things. Sometimes, anyway. On one ordinary morning, he was with his father on the shore, readying the nets, lost in a daydream, when a voice called to him.

"Come follow me."

A rabbi. But how? He'd failed to ascend the spiritual schools and become apprentice to a spiritual teacher. Here he was, his sandals wet, their leather cracking, the smell of fish forever permeating his tunic. But there was the rabbi, calling, "Come follow me. Be my student."

So, he followed. To be apprentice to a teacher? To capture the imaginations of men rather than capture fish? How could he not follow? He listened closely, but his rabbi was often mysterious, sometimes enigmatic—a man of strange and difficult teachings. But something else too. A compelling majesty emanated from him.

All other religious leaders the boy had ever known taught as proxies to a tradition. They taught on behalf of the order to which they belonged—and the order functioned only as emissary to The Name, Hashem, GOD, all-powerful righteousness and authority. But the boy's teacher—though he reverenced God as much and more so than any spiritual leader the boy had ever known—called God, *Dad*. The teacher taught not as an envoy to the truth but as if he held all authority on truth itself, in and of himself. And the boy was not alone in noticing this. As the boy followed the teacher, others came to follow as well. Dozens, then hundreds, then thousands came just to hear him speak. The teacher stood at the center of the great rolling crowd on a hill and talked about God. The teacher awed the people, and the boy couldn't help but feel proud to be his student.

The teacher looked out on the eager throng of would-be followers and called only twelve to follow him always, in closest intimacy, to be more than students, to be friends. And the boy listened, his heart hammering against his ribs, as the teacher listed them off, one by one, and then the teacher said his name. The boy went and stood with the others. He looked at the teacher, smiling, and realized then that what he felt was more than admiration. He loved the teacher as one loves a brother, a father, a friend.

Day by day, weeks into months, he followed the teacher. What began as a wonderful invitation became incredible, vivifying mentorship, then became something more. The teacher placed his hands on sick people and made them well. The teacher found those whose lives had been laid waste by disease and demons and madness, and the teacher merely spoke, and the sickness, demons, and despair ran from the ailing and aggrieved as if fleeing the teacher's presence, as if in terror, and those so lowly as to have been cast out even by their own people were, in a moment, restored.

One afternoon, as the boy watched, he allowed himself to consider for the first time a question he'd been too afraid to ask. Could the teacher be the king? He sat by a fire one night with the other eleven apprentices, his best friends, and, lost in his own familiar imagination, he envisioned the teacher raising his sword to the western sky, bisecting the sun. He imagined the teacher's now-familiar voice calling out, the awe-inspiring authority in it, infectious courage permeating a crowd of thousands as they prepared to bring evil to an end. But then the boy dared to move the daydream forward. He saw in his mind the teacher taking the promised throne of Israel, the teacher as the king, and he saw himself there with him. And he knew then in his heart that whatever fear and hardship lay before them on the teacher's journey to the throne, he would go with him and fight by his side and be his servant and his friend.

One night, all of them huddled in a boat on the waters when a storm befell them. He forgot his courage then and cried, for he was afraid. He shook the teacher from sleep, baffled by his indifference as the boat threatened to topple. "Save us!" he remembered saying, later embarrassed by his panic and desperation. He hadn't even known what the teacher could do to keep the boat from sinking, the twelve of them from drowning, but wasn't the teacher their leader? Shouldn't he do something? And the teacher had stood facing the storm and the sea, and he just … told it to be quiet. And the storm listened.

The boy was terrified then to see power like this. And he knew—he *knew* the teacher was the king, but felt also that he was more, though not knowing what *more* could be—and he was afraid.

The boy had followed the teacher for years when the teacher began to speak of death and dying. The boy knew, of course, of all the other would-be kings to come and go across the long, miserable timeline of his people's suffering—those hopeful messiah figures who'd roused hearts and minds and led doomed rebellions against the oppressors and their empires, who had been imprisoned or even beheaded for their troubles. To hear the teacher talk about dying conjured these images in the boy's mind—and he hated them. He thought, *I am only misunderstanding the teacher, who,* he reminded himself, *often speaks in riddles and gruesome metaphors.* After all, the teacher had spoken of self-mutilation—to pluck out your eye or lop off your limbs if they cause you to sin—and he'd not actually required any of the twelve to follow through on these terrible decrees. He was just like that, the teacher, strange and intense, and the boy had often resigned himself to failure at interpreting some of the teacher's riddles, accepting this as a limitation of his own acumen and having nothing to do with any shortcoming in the teacher's masterful rhetoric.

One day as they walked, the teacher asked him pointedly, "Who do you think I am, really?" And the boy, heat burning in his temples, his pace quickening, just blurted it out.

"You are the king. And more."

He almost couldn't believe he'd said it out loud like that, and it felt dangerous loosed into the air, wild and uncensored, but he was more convinced of its truth than ever before as the words hung in the air around him. The teacher smiled at him then. He put his hand on the boy's shoulder and told the boy he was right, that this truth was a blessing from God, that the teacher—no, the king—would build his entire rebellion of hope on these words spoken by this poor, fish-stinking boy he'd called to follow him years prior.

The boy loved him completely—his teacher, his master, his friend.

A baleful sense hung in the air—something heavy among them—as they walked to the great city. Something was nigh, something coming to completion, something hidden in the teacher's cryptic mentions of death—a secret, a metaphor, the moment finally at hand.

The boy was ready.

The night came for them to observe the most sacred of spiritual occasions together, the Passover dinner. The teacher seemed somehow different. Sadness tinged his voice and pulled on his face. He spoke of broken bodies and spilled blood, and the boy was afraid. Sitting at the table, he remembered his vision of the teacher with his sword raised, ready to lead them in righteous revolt against evil, his eyes set on the throne eternal. But the teacher broke the spell of the boy's daydream with his strange talk of death. And the boy realized his love for the teacher had become so profound, so complete, that he wanted to go with him even if their rebellion against evil ended in defeat. He told the teacher so. "I'd die with you tonight," he said, meaning every word. But the teacher rebuked him. Didn't believe him. Said the boy would betray him. The boy was confused and hurting when they went outside to pray, and when soldiers arrived under torches in the night to arrest the teacher—no, the king—the boy's mouth hung open in disbelieving panic.

He knew the time had come. It wasn't the way he'd pictured it, but it had come nonetheless, and now he would do more than walk with his king into the throne room; he would be the one to rescue the king from his would-be captors! The boy drew a sword, wild, frenzied, and swung at the head of the soldier seizing his teacher and king, just missing, catching and severing the evildoer's ear. The boy screamed at the others, calling them to uprising, but the teacher rebuked him again. And the teacher put his hand on the injured soldier the way he'd touched the sick and the oppressed, and he healed him. The teacher, the king, went away with the soldiers willingly, quietly.

The boy was not ready to forfeit the plan. The teacher was mysterious, he reminded himself. The teacher often surprised them. Almost every day, he surprised them! So, the boy crept behind them at a distance, waiting anxiously for some misunderstanding to be relieved, some new truth to be uncovered, for the images of his vision to come to life before his very eyes. Instead, he watched as the soldiers beat and battered and spit on the teacher, his friend. The teacher looked helpless before them and did nothing to quell their violence against him.

The boy winced, his heart and body shuddering, his stomach turning each time they struck his friend, tears stinging his eyes, his teeth gritted with such pressure he thought they might crack. The soldiers brought the teacher before a mock trial, a sinister pantomime, and the boy listened as they lobbed ridiculous accusations against him, things verifiably untrue, in an assured and precluded effort to obtrude their selfish will against him. After all, the teacher had not played by the rules of the religious leaders, had demonstrated the terrible audacity to name their corruptions and rebuke the injustice of their legalism, empty religiousness, and greed—the same evils that had driven Israel into exile generations prior.

And the teacher had claimed to be a king. Treason. If the oppressors knew, they could treat him like all the other would-be messiahs. Imprisonment. Death. The religious leaders, the boy could see, were manipulating the narrative, making the teacher out to be like all the other doomed false messiahs so the empire would dispose of him and silence his challenge against their way of life. But why did the teacher not speak? Why did he not rebuke them? Not defend himself? The teacher hardly said anything at all until one of the religious leaders leaned into his face and charged him, "Are you the promised king?" The boy tensed where he watched from a distance, practically willing his friend to say no, to buy some time, to refuse to dignify this ridiculousness with the truth.

But the teacher assented. "I am the king," he said. "And I am more. I am God." At this, his accusers cried out. What further testimony was necessary to put the teacher to death? None. The boy was afraid.

Someone appeared beside him. "Weren't you with him? The one they are accusing? Aren't you one of his students?"

The boy couldn't say why he said it. He just blurted it out: "No!" And the word seared his heart as it came. He stumbled backward then, fear becoming horror as they struck and spit on his friend in the distance—the once-magnetic teacher who captured the hearts and minds of thousands with his words and presence and miracles, now looking like a sad rag doll, bullied and helpless.

Someone else sidled up to the boy. "You're one of his, aren't you? One of the rabbi's students. You were with him."

And again, the awful words spilled from the boy like vomit. "No, I wasn't. Not me."

They were leading the teacher out now, already battered, in chains, tears in his eyes. The boy had lost any grip on his vision of the triumphant king; he was so afraid. In the uproar, the chants of condemnation, the pummeling of the teacher's sad visage, the boy wanted to run, to get away from all this; panic had overcome his rationale. Someone else was at his side again, "I know you were with him. You even talk like him."

The words poured from the boy like poison then, his only urge the primal scramble to survive, a spider skittering backward to avoid a foot. He said he wasn't with the teacher, that he didn't even know the man at all; he called down obscenities and oaths to utterly renounce the teacher, swearing he was a stranger. When he'd finished his mad tirade, the boy turned, panting, and saw the teacher just feet away, looking into his eyes, having heard every word.

The boy ran. And he wept.

Later, the boy heard rumblings, whispers that gave way to a bloodcurdling chorus. *Crucify.* Surely, such a horror was impossible for a man whose only crime was offending religious leaders. Imprisonment, the boy knew, was a possibility. Even execution, he admitted, he had considered briefly in moments of cold dread, but to be crucified? A heinous torture, the ultimate indignity, a barbarism so inhumane even those who carried it out it frowned upon it. This was madness.

But they did everything they said they would. They beat the teacher within an inch of his life; his flesh hung from his body in bloodied ribbons. The face of the man the boy had loved as his closest friend and master swelled beyond recognition. They stripped him naked in front of everyone and hammered nails through his hands and feet with other common criminals, then left him to die on the cross from sepsis or shock or asphyxiation—whichever came first.

But the boy's great shame was that he wasn't even there.

All of them ran in the night when the soldiers came. All twelve. They were so scared. But one of the twelve, he went back and was there with Jesus as he died. Another of the master's disciples, Mary, had stayed with him too, with some of the other women. So did Jesus' mom. But the boy only hid and cried. He'd been pathetic, hollowed out by fear, and he hated himself for it. His friend Judas had been the one to tell the soldiers where to find the teacher, and Judas, so overcome with regret and despair, killed himself.

The boy was empty then. For the first time in years, he walked home knowing the well of hope had finally gone completely dry. Cold and defeated, the boy woke in the morning and followed his father back to the boat to fish. The boy's name was Simon, but the master had called him Peter. "The rock." But the boy had crumbled. For him, the story was over.

Some of the women who had followed the teacher got up early to visit his tomb, but the boy did not go with them. He thought of the last time he'd seen the teacher, their eyes locked in an awful moment where part of the boy was still trapped, a moment he worried would last forever. But the women returned in hysterics, babbling nonsense, going on about the how stone that covered the tomb had been moved, about men in bright clothes, that the teacher's body was gone. The others asked questions, attempted to calm the women, but the boy's eyes went wide. While they were still talking, he stood, something grasping his heart, and he ran.

He ran all the way to the teacher's tomb. The stone covering the entrance was indeed rolled back. Panting, sweat beaded on his arms and forehead, the boy ducked into the dark doorway cut in the rock face. Shafts of daylight bathed the grave slab, an amber glow. Strips of linen lay on the stone, but no corpse. Had someone stolen the teacher's body? Had he been moved? His brow furrowed in confusion the entire walk home, sweat cooling his body to a shiver.

In the morning, he went out to fish again, as empty as he had ever felt in his life. Some of his friends, other apprentices of the teacher, came with him, not knowing what to do with themselves, really. They fished for hours and caught nothing, a terrible metaphor for the great tragedy of their lives. A man called to them from the beach, something about casting nets on the right side of the boat. In their exhaustion, they obliged the stranger for no other reason but numb resignation. The lowered nets almost instantly filled with fish. So many fish that the boat listed from the weight of them, writhing in the net, their glistening grey bellies turned up to the sky.

The boy scowled at the haul, flummoxed. There was something familiar in the strangeness of this exchange. One of the boy's friends looked at the bulging net, then to the stranger on the beach, then to the boy, and said, "It's *him*."

The boy leapt into the water. He swam toward the stranger and the shore the way he'd run to the tomb, but when he hauled himself up on the beach, sodden and breathless, he found not discarded linens and an empty grave but the teacher. He was alive.

They sat on the beach together. Three times the teacher asked, "Do you love me?" And three times the boy answered, "Yes." He was hurt that the teacher asked him again and again. He didn't realize then that the teacher was taking each of the boy's terrible failures and undoing them. Three times, the boy denied knowing the teacher, but there on the beach, three times he loved him, and the teacher allowed love to have the final word. The moment of shame and regret the boy feared would last forever came to an end that morning on the beach. And the teacher told the boy, as he had done the day they met, "Follow me."

After that day, it wasn't that the boy was never afraid again, but something about what he did when he was afraid changed. He didn't fish anymore. He went back to traveling. He told everyone what he'd seen, what had happened. He told them about his magnificent failures, about the cross, about the abandoned linens and the empty tomb, and about what had happened on the beach. He didn't really care what happened to him anymore—if he got in trouble—only that the world knew the truth. The tomb was empty. The teacher was the king after all. He was more than that. He was God.

Sometimes the boy, Peter, was put in prison, or whipped, or mocked, and he surprised himself with his own persistence. He kept it up. How could he not? Eventually, Peter was arrested for the last time and nailed to a cross, like his teacher before him. Follow me, the teacher had said, and the boy had obeyed. He asked that they hang him upside down. To mirror his teacher in death so precisely was an honor of which the boy did not consider himself worthy. The boy who was once too afraid to admit he'd been seen with the teacher became the man who pleaded to be hung upside down.

As Peter was being fastened to the cross he'd once so despised, he did not cry out, "It was a lie! The tomb was not empty!" Instead, he said, "No, don't hang me upright. I'm not worthy to die like he did. The tomb is empty."

The world, for centuries, has puzzled for an answer that many know full well and believe deep down in their very bones. How else can it be true unless the tomb was empty? Though we did not see it with our eyes, we see it with our hearts: the tomb is empty. It still is! It always will be! The tomb is empty forever and ever. And all of us who believe this, we believe it, shaking, doubting and fretful as we often are, just like that boy did and does. Aren't we all failures like he was? Haven't all of us said, in word and in deed, that we didn't know him? That we wanted no part of him? And didn't he call to us on the beach after we did it, and didn't he love us anyway?

No other God in the world or in history loves, suffers, and dies for traitors and hypocrites. That boy, Peter, finally did see his teacher become king. But not with the military might of his daydreams. Instead, the king rose from poverty, no sword in his hand at all, and stretched out both arms in the western sky, bisecting the sun—the king who reminded his people of their long winter of suffering and proclaimed the end was nigh. He led his warriors triumphant into the heart of darkness, and defeating death and hell, he cut down the enemy presence that had grown cancerous in the world. With the love of his people burning in his chest, the king destroyed this wickedness, took his rightful place on the throne God prepared for him as a promise to his people before he'd ever been born—but his throne was the cross.

And when he rose, the last dregs of hope in a well reduced to dust became an ocean that overflows and replenishes a land once barren. And it overflows forever and ever because he is raised. Because he is with us. And you. And me. All of us sniveling screw-ups doomed to the same living and dying as everyone before us, we are not left to scramble after a mighty yet aloof god—a god who could never know our suffering—a god with love so infirm as to be conditional, who demands righteous works and good behavior and enlightenment for clearance, for paradise, for transcendence. No. The all-powerful God is the God of love. From eternity past, he loved, and for eternity on, he loves. The Father, the Son, and the Spirit.

Jesus: the way, the truth, and the life. No one comes to God except through Jesus. No one comes to God except through the cross and the empty tomb. And God has come low to us to save us, we who did nothing and do nothing to deserve it. How could we? His grace was always going before us, in front of us, ready to forgive us, to love us. And if he loved us unto death and that was the end, that would be a beautiful, remarkable story, but it would be a tragedy. The movement of Jesus across centuries and the globe is not built on a tragedy. The story did not and does not end in death.

Though we did not see it with our eyes, we see it with our hearts: the tomb is empty. It still is! It always will be! The tomb is empty forever and ever, amen, amen. The well continues to overflow. It overflows eternal. Forever and ever, amen.

V. ON CATHEDRALS AND CHAOS

FIRST, THERE WERE TWELVE, but the twelve told others the good news. The twelve saw Jesus raised, and the twelve were filled with the Holy Spirit—the same Spirit who raised their master from the dead—just as their master promised they would be. They told the good news in word and in deed—with speeches and sermons, they told it. Before crowds and around dinner tables, they told it. With justice and mercy, they told it. With miracles, signs, and wonders, they told it.

Twelve became hundreds, became thousands. It wasn't safe, proclaiming a new kingdom and a new king in necessary defiance of the old king and his old kingdom. So they were arrested, flogged, and executed, but they wouldn't stop telling or living the good news. The movement spread throughout homes and communities, across villages and regions, undeterred by the constant looming threat of persecution and death.

It went on like this for hundreds of years until a strange epiphany entered the mind of a Roman emperor. Shrewd and forward-looking, he peered out on an ever-growing movement and declared it, for the first time, legal. Now, the master's apprentices need not gather in secret nor live with the burden of likely and imminent punishment for sharing and living the good news. The emperor, hungry for power and thirsty for blood, required his metallurgists to forge Christian symbols into his weapons of warfare, and for the first time in hundreds of years, a movement of peasants and pacifists went the way of powerful warlords. Corruption had always infected the movement, but the movement itself was not corrupt. It was carried on by imperfect apprentices, as it always had been. And now, the movement was growing. Official councils were formed to organize and clarify precious Christian doctrine in keeping with the master's teaching and with the good news as it was handed down by the twelve. Creeds were written and recited.

A new emperor came. He imposed the movement on all the empire—an official civil religion—and he split the empire in two, the East and the West. Political and theological disagreements further separated the two regions. But Rome eventually fell, as empires do, and a new, anti-Christian religion emerged from Arabia and proliferated. Amidst this hostile geopolitical storm, the movement in the East split definitively from the movement in the West, a great schism, leading to centuries of violent warfare in the name of a master who had forbidden all violence. People were, as they were in the beginning, broken.

The primitive (and then slightly less primitive) human being bumbling and staggering along the road of discipleship, many of them falling away like they always have.

Some who led the church held the truth of the Scriptures captive in languages unspoken by the poor and uneducated. Some in the church began to charge sinners for the forgiveness of sins, further solidifying a barrier between God and people that could only be crossed by rich and powerful religious leaders on their behalf—the very evil so severely condemned by the master himself.

A German priest rebelled. He was joined by priests in France and Switzerland, and a new strand of the movement emerged, free from oppressive bureaucracy or spiritual taxation. Without centralized or officially recognized governance, this new strand further splintered into dozens of unique expressions and denominations, and eventually, colonists from northern Europe carried these outgrowths to what we now know as America and began to establish churches there.

Those churches planted other churches. Some of them resembled expressions carried out in cathedrals, others were like communities gathered around dinner tables. Some of them practiced liturgies and sacraments from the West, others the East. Some of them carried on the traditions of the protesting priests from Germany, from France, from Switzerland. In all expressions and traditions, there were mistakes and corruptions because all of them were carried out by human beings. But in many of those same churches, imperfect though they were, there were apprentices who struggled against their own failures to practice and preach Christian doctrine in keeping with the master's teaching and with the good news as it was handed down by the twelve. They've been living out a series of deaths, the old self becoming something new. They've done beautiful things and ugly things, gotten it right and gotten it wrong, crawled into caves, chained themselves to stones.

For hundreds of years, they've been telling stories about temples and kings, about mountains and miracles, stories about parted seas and freed slaves and old widows redeemed and the master who was crucified, died, was buried, then rose again, conquering death and hell forever. For hundreds of years, they have been filled with the Holy Spirit—the same Spirit who raised their master from the dead—just as their master promised they would be. By the Spirit, they continue to tell the story of Jesus by doing justice, healing the sick, driving out demons. For all their failures and deficiencies, they continue to walk behind the master, to carry out life within the sacred community of the church.

Hundreds of years later, a pastor of one such church wrote a book about the beginning and the end and about the kinds of things apprentices do between them. Someone is reading that book now, deciding again and again if they will follow the master to the next death.

VI. A LITANY AGAINST DEATH

I WAS BORN NAKED and screaming, but even then, God was there. Before me. Before my cells took shape, before they split, God was there. Before wars waged by man, before the poison of puff adders and the twitching antennae of the thrumming cicada, there was the one true and triune God—the Father, the Son, and the Holy Spirit. The one and only God over all in three distinct persons, each of them sharing one divine essence, substance, and nature.

God's core identity is neither creator nor ruler, for he requires neither creation nor subjects to realize his identity. Before he created, before he ruled, God was love. It was from an overflow of God's love that he created, and it is an outpouring of God's love from which he rules. God cannot do other than love. Even God's anger and indignation against evil and hell burn from the fire of his love. The sorrow and grief of God, the discipline and correction of God are all born from his love. It was an act of God's generous and self-sacrificial love that he imbued human and spiritual beings with self-government—that he allowed us a say. What love can there be if not freely chosen? God has invited us—not forced nor coerced us—into his eternal love. Most of the time, everyone declines.

Our rejection of God's love is our rejection of what is best in all things designed by the one who created all things. Chaos, violence, injustice, suffering, and death all boil over from the wellspring of humanity's destructive, self-seeking evil. Apart from the God who is loving goodness, we can be neither loving nor good.

So, we wreck things.

But God insisted on love, and God's love is not contingent on obedience or good behavior. He cannot help but love. God accomplished his rescue mission through Jesus of Nazareth—through his life, death, burial, and resurrection from the dead. To be saved from the awfulness of a broken world and the inevitable finality of dying, God requires no behavioral gymnastics, no money, no private program, no secret knowledge, no enlightenment. God's love is a gift freely given, and given first, before we loved him.

To accept the gift of God's love and salvation is to submit one's life to the lordship of Jesus, to whom all authority in heaven and on earth has been given. To follow Jesus as master is freedom; the freedom to live as God intended, all relationships—with self, others, and creation—flourishing. The apprentice of Jesus demonstrates love for him in obedience to his teaching, not to curry his favor nor earn his love, but to embody a relationship. The teaching of Jesus is contained within the inspired and authoritative Scriptures—breathed out by the very Spirit of God.

The Scriptures are not an antiquated byproduct of ancient religious ignorance but a mysterious and profound library written by many human authors and one divine author. The Scriptures will not bend to modern sensibilities; they remain the most sophisticated work of literary artistry in the history of the written word. In them is the truth. The student of Jesus enters the lifelong process of reading and contemplating the Scriptures to interpret them within the accountability of God's people— centuries of sages and scholars young and old from all over the world—and to put their teachings into practice. Obedience to the teaching of Jesus recorded in the delegated authority of the Scriptures does not conjure God's love, as if the love of God were a sad and emaciated thing that required chores just to will itself into existence. Obedience to Jesus is freedom and life to the fullest. Jesus will come again to set the world right.

I was born naked and screaming, but even then, God was there. God is still here. Emmanuel. God with us.

PARABLE: THE STUPID SHEEP

I OFTEN LOSE MY way, but never so bad as that day. The herd was feeding. So many sheep. Uncountable. I wandered the boundary, chewing grass. I was smaller than the others. I escaped their notice. So many of them eating, all vying for the same space, the same grass. The shepherd watched over the herd, not over me. He sat on the sloping hillside, watching. The ground went dark in the gloaming as I wandered between two arching tree trunks, bowed to the right and the left, the space between them like a doorway to the wood. I went in, my appetites steering me to find my own space to feed.

Shafts of light breaking through the treetops overhead dimmed and disappeared. The sound of my hooves in the loam eclipsed by a cacophony of insects, hooting birds, breathing shadows. A fear set in, tiny but palpable, a flicker of panic. I went back the way I came but could not find the arching trees—the doorway in and out of the wood. Had I taken a different path backward? How far had I wandered? A pain in my leg, my hoof against a knot of roots growing tumor-like from the dirt. I fell. My back leg had become snared in a thorny bramble. I pulled and pulled, but the ropey vine only constricted. With my front legs, I kicked and struggled, digging trenches in the ground.

Then the terrible racket of the forest rose all around me: skittering claws on tree trunks, a howl in the distance, something wheezing and drooling in the dark. My heart hammered against my ribs, and I thought of the shepherd then. I bleated despite myself, foolishly summoning whatever thing with fangs and claws lurked in nearby darkness.

Then a lantern light split the shadows, and the shepherd was there, his arm outstretched, the flame dangling in his grasp, his gaze focused and searching. My breath was shallow and ragged when I saw him, and I realized I was no longer kicking or bleating. He kneeled beside me, there in the dirt, and with deft movements snapped my entanglements with one hand, the other resting gently against my face. He kept saying, "I'm here. I'm here." And he lifted me onto his shoulders and carried me through the dark until we'd left the forest and returned home, where the herd—the enormous scope of it—waited, a great white throng of sheep stretching out across the hillside. He'd left all of them to come find me.

THE NICENE CREED

I believe in one God,

the Father almighty,

maker of heaven and earth,

of all things visible and invisible.

I believe in one Lord Jesus Christ,

the Only Begotten Son of God,

born of the Father before all ages.

God from God, Light from Light,

true God from true God,

begotten, not made, consubstantial with
     the Father;

through him all things were made.

For us men and for our salvation

he came down from heaven,

and by the Holy Spirit was incarnate of the
    Virgin Mary,

and became man.

For our sake he was crucified under Pontius
    Pilate,

he suffered death and was buried,

and rose again on the third day

in accordance with the Scriptures.

He ascended into heaven

and is seated at the right hand of the Father.

He will come again in glory

to judge the living and the dead

and his kingdom will have no end.

I believe in the Holy Spirit, the Lord, the giver
    of life,

who proceeds from the Father and the Son,

who with the Father and the Son is adored
    and glorified,

who has spoken through the prophets.

I believe in one holy universal and apostolic
    Church.

I confess one Baptism for the forgiveness
    of sins

and I look forward to the resurrection of
    the dead

and the life of the world to come. Amen.

BOOK TWO: THE HARROWING OF HELL

PARABLE

———

A NOTE FROM
THE AUTHOR

———

I.–XVIII. THE
MASTER'S TEACHING

"If they were born with these afflictions, he should recite the blessing 'Blessed are You, God, our Lord, King of the universe, who has altered His creations.'"

MISHNEH TORAH, BLESSINGS 10:12

"The way of the transgressor is hard.
God made this world, but he didn't
make it to suit everybody, did he?"

CORMAC MCCARTHY, *Blood Meridian*

PARABLE: THE DEFIANT GARDEN

EVERY MORNING I watch a strange gardener from my kitchen window. He gardens out of chaos. One morning, he went strolling in his yard while the dew still beaded the grass. He looked down on a wild arena of bramble, stone, and dirt, and he reached tenderly into his bag of seeds, scattering big handfuls of them in every direction. I watched, frowning, unable to make any sense of it. I saw him water all of it, and for days afterward, I squinted into his yard from my kitchen window, looking for buds I knew would never grow to adulthood.

The ravens came first, gobbling up every seed that had tumbled onto the sidewalk beyond the yard. The heat wave came next, burning up the first tender sprouts to erupt from shallow soil. Most of the plants that became seedlings were entangled with dandelions and briars, powerful and parasitic, and they wilted, drooped, and fell.

But months after it all began, some of the seeds to escape the ravens, the rocks, the sun, and the weeds, they twisted into the air above the soil, unfurling long branches that eventually sagged with ripened fruit and budding flowers. The fruit tumbled from the branches and split in the soil, and the glistening seeds within brought forth more sprouts and seedlings and plants until the gardener's yard was overrun with them. Journalists and experts came from all over the world to observe, astonished, and they took photographs and leaf samples. They'd say to one another, "Incredible! Look at how the garden grows!" Knowing nothing of the ravens and thorns.

THE RAVEN AND THE PALM TREE

ON A TRIP TO Palm Desert when I was nearly forty-one, I observed a raven in a palm tree. It was June, more than one hundred degrees outside, the sky blue and cloudless. The raven looped in the air above the swimming pool, cawing, eventually landing in the green fronds fanning out from a treetop that extended cartoon-like some forty or fifty feet overhead. I was blinking chlorinated water out of my eyes when I saw it, the sight of the bird interrupting pool games with my kids and my slow sips from a cold seltzer water. I lifted the sunglasses from my head to see the bird where it perched, ominous but unthreatening.

It was my smallest child, Arlo, who most centered me on that trip, his gleeful contentment with wrestling and tickling, and

I remember a moment one afternoon when I looked up from a book I'd been reading and wondered, *Why do I feel far from myself?* Not sad, not discontented at all, really, but not present to the Spirit of God without concentrated effort. Sometimes, not even with effort. *How long have I been doing this,* I thought, *only to find myself struggling from time to time?*

When I first set out to write this book, I tried desperately to extricate myself from its pages, but the more I wrote, the less I knew how to excuse myself from its story. I worried that including myself in a book like this might anchor it in a kind of specificity unaccommodating to you, the reader; that my thoughts and stories might prove unrelatable, muddying the truth I hope to spread across these pages. It's not a book about me, after all.

But in a certain sense, all of us are more or less the same, give or take. All of us go on reaching into the cold infinite void with trembling hands in hopes of the something we all know— somehow, deep down, know—is out there. This *something*, whatever it is, we figure we really need, but we're also terrified by the prospect of finding it. If we find it, we know things will change. And oh, the terrible irony that the something beyond and within all this is not to be feared at all. No, it casts out all fear forever. But change is scary. A young man told me this in my office one afternoon. He was on the precipice of disciple-ship, unwilling to budge. I asked him why. "What's keeping you? Why wait? You're right there. Step over the edge."

"I'm afraid," he told me. "If I say, 'Jesus is king,' he's going to change things." I shrugged. This was true.

"Things are changing one way or another," I said. As I write this, the young man hasn't budged.

"Maybe," some have said, "if I'd been born some other time or place, I'd have been beholden to other gods and their laws and customs and temples," but I wasn't and I'm not. And had I been born to these other gods, desperate for their approval via righteous works or sacrifices or money or bloodshed, all my hope in reincarnation or enlightenment or paradise or some celestial kingdom with me in charge, my wretchedness would only rebound on the impenetrable carapace of the void, unresolved. But I was pursued by the God of love, the only God of love, the only God who dies to spare the wretched a death they deserve.

It's not that everything is always so awful, really. But even the best of things suffers a vandalizing black blot if you zoom out enough to see it—a raven in a palm tree. Even when we're doing really well, our insides are entangled in our brokenness. Even when things are going really well, suffering creeps around some corner, waiting to pounce. Even a very good story is barreling toward death. Everyone wants to stop or at least slow down, but someone cut the brakes. Someone planted weeds in the garden.

I was still hoping for some way out of these pages that afternoon in the desert, before I saw the raven. After that, I went inside, started typing, and found myself in the words as they came. These things I write, I write them as a kind of mission. God has not, to date, summoned me to some country beyond my home armed with little more than the gospel and my wits. He has not, to date, entrusted me with a charitable nonprofit or a clinic for lepers. Instead, he has given me words and then typewriters with which to commit and entrust them, and these words I commit and entrust to you. They are what I have been given, and I am giving them to you. You are the beloved of God.

I. GOOD NEWS FOR WORTHLESS PEOPLE!

GOD IS NOW AVAILABLE to humanity. You have access to the creative and personal power behind the universe's construction. The one true God over all wants to know you. You: the spiritually bankrupt. The religiously deprived and theologically uneducated. The spiritual zeros. You who wear no badge of churchy esteem, with no wealth of pious experience nor any sacred clout to speak of. Good news for those who have never cracked a Bible and never warmed a church pew. For those who don't know how to pray out loud or to speak the secret language of the spiritual performance artist.

God himself says, "Welcome."

The king is personally inviting you into the kingdom. To those at the end of their proverbial rope: God chooses you. The wife abandoned by her husband. The widower weeping into the empty space where his wife once slept. God is calling. You parents who have buried your children and you children who have buried your parents, God sees you. To each and every one of you laid waste by life's merciless bulldozer of grief, God says, "I have comfort for you."

For every timid, waffling, nervous wreck of reluctance and indecision, God is inviting you to the front of the line. For most of your life, your voice has gone unheard as the words freeze in your throat. You seem to shrink against the turbulent backdrop of humanity—neglected, overlooked, disregarded. God holds you in the highest esteem! Your smallness is big to God. Though you have become convinced of your insignificance, God stands poised to hand over the keys to his kingdom.

I have hope for the horribly wronged. For those who have beaten the seemingly impenetrable wall of the world's injustice with defiant fists. God says, "I am coming to make things right." For you, life has become criminally unfair. Where thieves and murderers oppress the vulnerable and destroy the weak, where the powerful prey on the powerless, know this: the very flame of their evil will be snuffed out once and for all as injustice itself crumbles before the relentless love of God.

Let those whose compassion has been called weakness celebrate! God sees all the kindness the world deems foolish. Though you have been called a doormat, an enabler, naïve, God has set you up as an example for the selfish and stingy. You who know all too well what it means to give until it hurts. You've emptied your wallets, your emotional strength, your psychological depth to care for the undeserving. Well, God is going to do the same for you.

God is going to do even more.

And you poor, poor perfectionists! How you drive the world and yourselves insane as everything around you fails to measure up. You for whom the food never tastes right, the temperature never accommodates, your surroundings never satisfy. The world simply fails to perform, and you sit chief amongst its great failures, ever the disappointment, a frowning visage of malcontent in every reflective surface. You, my friend, are going to see God. For you, the not-good-enough will become the better-than-you-could-have-ever-imagined.

Those frustrating intermediaries who advocate peace in the face of a world ravenous for war—God relates to you. You double-minded men and women who insist on seeing both sides, on reaching for empathy rather than swift justice—how you vex the volatile. Standing arms outstretched in between squabble after squabble, no one trusts you who sympathize with the ungrateful and the wicked. The God who does good even to those in the wrong sees you.

I have a comforting word for every person who has been cut down because of his or her concern for what is right. You who reject the world's guns, the world's wars, the violence of word and fist, you who favor peace in a world inflamed for power— one day, the world will see that you are like God himself.

You who refuse to depart from what you know to be right even in the face of overwhelming opposition. You've been called names, refused work, fired from your job, locked up in prison, rejected, dejected, dismissed, and denounced. God is making available to you a reality in which no ultimate harm can find you. You will reign in God's kingdom.

It doesn't end there! On and on the invitation unfolds before us all like a scroll without end. Watch it unfurl as it speeds past the undesirable and inconvenient—and written across this scroll again and again, a banner utterly offensive to the privileged and well-to-do: I have good news for worthless people!

At God's party, the toothless vagrant—babbling and stinking of urine—goes dancing to the seat of honor as the prim and prestigious are kindly asked to move aside. The uneducated, the dropouts, the welfare recipients, and the trailer trash are all awarded crowns and asked to sit with God himself. Every one of you billions scraping through this unforgiving life each day with little more than pennies in your shaking, hungry hands, God is going to stand you proudly before the fat and wealthy. God is going to give you the future. Every sallow weakling, dying on your sterile hospital bed, wax skin stretched over quivering ribs as sickness devours your body, as disease parades through your blood cells, God is going to come close to you. God is going to wrap his arms around you. You will feel God's touch with a profound intimacy unknown to those whose bodies have not been run through by disease, whose minds have not been tainted by the madness of suffering.

God has a plan to set the world right. To do so, he would like to use illegal immigrants and refugees. God would like to enlist the displaced family crowded into their studio apartment, desperate for work, for hope, for a future. God himself will give them all three. To those who have been told, "No, not you," God says, "Yes, you."

God is coming to rescue the disabled and disfigured. Those unable to walk, or speak, or see, or think—they are the apples of God's eye. Today they have become royalty.

Oh you foster kids and abused children, unloved and passed around and punished beneath the hands and fists of the evil and unkind: You have been adopted by God. Yes, God has cleared his schedule to meet with you. The most pressing affairs of the entire universe God readily drops to the floor to open his arms before you. God will lift you up in his embrace. He will kiss your face and celebrate you before the world. Head over heels, he loves you!

Yes, you. The lonely, the awkward, the unbearable, the ugly, the too fat, the too thin, and the unimpressive failures. The weirdos, the bullied, the too proud, the too scared, the single moms, the divorcées, the corrupt and twisted out of shape, the hopelessly overwhelmed, and the overwhelmingly hopeless.

The majesty and strength of God's everlasting kingdom begin today with you. Through you, the light of God's goodness will shine bright, and no darkness can obscure it.

I have very good news for you.

118

II. THE MISSING ABOLITION

ONCE, GOD WROTE WISDOM on stone. That wisdom—that *teaching*—was given to God's people as a light shining in the darkness. Thousands of years before this book, after that Israelite woman walked on dry land through the parted sea, she and her people would wait at the foot of Mount Sinai as a man called Moses carried that stone wisdom down from the summit. When he came, he found a waiting people already curdled by evil. He was so frustrated by the inevitability of human failure that he threw the stone, and the stone shattered. It's the same old story, really.

We're not always so great with wisdom and words. People, I mean. Our souls want for poetry and secrets, but our minds reach for facts and figures, and we can imagine no world in which the two are interlaced and the child of their pairing is the truth. Usually, when presented with a mystery, we try to twist it into the shape of a fact and vice versa. Once, God wrote wisdom on stone. It wasn't an exhaustive, detailed manual on all possible and proper human behaviors, but a glimpse into life well lived by the one who made life. Across centuries and authors and languages and continents, the story of God—breathed out by the Spirit into the hearts and minds of human authors—was committed to scrolls.

If God had elected to disclose himself to humanity, a story would be how he'd do it. He's wired our brains for stories, and stories resonate in the sacred sensibility of our souls more than diagrams and tidy sums. *Story* doesn't mean "not true." *Story* doesn't mean "make-believe." The story of God is wonderfully, complicatedly true. And within its winding intricacies are poems and parables, histories and hierarchies, rules and regulations, conviction and commandments. And across centuries and authors and languages and continents, it's all true. Thousands of years after God etched wisdom in stone, after the story had been preserved on sacred scrolls, a man stood on a mount with another teaching.

"I will not undo the story," Jesus said. It cannot be undone. Not a single dot of an *i* will be done away with, not one cross of a *t*. No detail, no aspect, no hook on a letter is going anywhere. Jesus said, "I haven't come to contradict a single poem or parable. I will not," Jesus assured, "abolish any command, nor contradict anything the Scriptures decree. I've come to fill them up," he said. "In fact, if *anyone* relaxes even the most seemingly small of these stories and statutes and decrees, their faith will be revealed to be the thing that is actually small.

"The whole story," Jesus said, "has been heading here, to me. I fill it full." The story to date is a staircase closing the gap between God and humanity that yawned open in the wake of human rebellion and evil. But the staircase could never reach God. It climbs higher and higher and ends with God yet in the distance until Jesus fills the story full, mends the staircase, and closes the gap.

My kids love to play outside. Our home is situated within a small, ordinary neighborhood on a quiet, unassuming street. Sometimes, a stranger barrels through, oblivious to the calm my neighbors and I take for granted. These cars, maybe lost or detoured, speed down our otherwise serene streets, provoking angry stares as they go.

Nothing separates my front yard from the street, and despite my insistence on the seriousness of my commands, when my children were very small, they saw no real reason to consistently obey my great decree to *stay away from the street*. To them, such an edict was arbitrary and confining. It existed only to restrict their freedom and pleasure. They could not yet conceive of a reality in which tiny bodies might be torn apart by speeding automobiles.

So, I corralled them further, limiting the scope of outdoor exploration, but still they wandered. So, I took them to the backyard, but still they snuck away. So, to protect them, I fenced them in. The backyard and the fence were not what either my wife or I envisioned but became necessary to protect them from death. Still, what I want for my kids, their lives, and their joy is much more than survival. There's much more.

That wisdom on stone, Jesus said, was like a fence. It served its purpose, but it was not and is not the vision of God for human flourishing, nor the true measure of God's love made manifest in the hearts, minds, and lives of his people. Jesus came to fulfill the story. For a story to be fulfilled, it could not be stripped for parts. The story could not be censored. The law in the stone could not be relaxed or scrubbed from its ancient surface.

Without the written Word, there can be no Way. The written Word is the delegated authority to which all apprentices are beholden. United in love for the master, we will neither defy nor deconstruct the written Word. We remain—like the mothers and fathers in the faith before us, the sisters and brothers who walk by our sides—submitted to the inspired, authoritative Word.

The Scriptures are binding. In all their ancient, mysterious, poetic, polarizing beauty, they are binding. We open their pages together, arm in arm with saints and sinners throughout the

II. THE MISSING ABOLITION

ages, committed to the lifelong work of study, meditation, and interpretation, and prepared to submit ourselves to their truth. Submission to the Word is neither clinical rule-keeping nor esoteric mysticism. Submission to the Word is obedience to the master. Obedience to the master is freedom.

III. THE PREAMBLE TO MURDER

MOST PEOPLE, WE CAN'T imagine a knife as a murder weapon. The danger of it occurs to us from time to time, but we go on slicing vegetables and opening cardboard boxes. Most people, statistically speaking, can't envision themselves on the firing side of an automatic weapon. Such a horror is reserved for Hollywood, for the marketable terrors of the twenty-four-hour news cycle. And maybe, for the murderer, it was once the same way.

But murder is not born into adulthood. Murder is conceived. It gestates, embryonic, and is birthed. Murder endures infancy, childhood, adolescence. Murder enters the world, as many evils do, in the devaluing and dehumanizing of someone else.

The trouble is that gentleness is kind to the world, but the world is not kind to gentleness. God will hold accountable the one who burns with anger, who seethes with animosity, because their anger vandalizes both themselves and the one their anger objectifies. The one who loses their temper against a brother or sister values themselves above another person made in God's image. They inflate themselves, fanning themselves out like a cobra's hood, and their words become their venom. The one who belittles another with words is—like the hateful and the murderer—one walking into destructive fire. The kind of fire that envelops waste and refuse and burns white-hot on the altars of demons where children are brought as sacrifices to detestable gods.

It is a viral contagion, anger. If you are preparing to meet with God and find its hooks somewhere within the hidden chambers of your heart, stop everything until they are unfastened, purged, and destroyed. Go to your brother. Go to your sister. Together, haul the terrible coiling darkness of anger up from within, that it might be burned away by the light of repentance and forgiveness and reconciliation. Walk a hundred miles to do it. Walk more. Leave everything behind.

Our politicians are angry. Our activists, celebrities, and CEOs are angry. We have been raised up on an illusion of anger as strength rather than weakness, as shrewd wisdom rather than disastrous foolishness. To prohibit murder alone fails to dignify human beings as God sees fit to dignify them. Let anger burn against evil and injustice itself, and let gentleness and peace reign in those who serve the master.

IV. WHEN TO GOUGE YOUR EYE OUT

WHEN A MAN GOES to a woman who is not his wife within the shadows of secrecy, when he puts his hands on her and braids his body into hers, he expresses the lechery of a creeping, inward evil once hidden away in the darkness of his soul and now made manifest with the darkness of his body.

God is the great architect of romance and sexuality. He made marriage up. Sexual desire, though an outworking of God-designed biological human mechanisms, is, like all desire, subject to the corruption of a world broken by sin. Sexual desire is never intrinsic to the identity of any human being. Who you are is not determined by who you want to have sex with, nor by having sex with them. No human being is made more human by expressing sexual desire, just as they are no less human if they don't express their sexuality at all. Jesus, our master, did not marry nor express his sexuality with a woman and is yet the greatest example of a fully integrated human being the world will ever know. Sexuality, then, is a powerful force capable of expressing redemption or damnation, depending. To govern this power, God designed the lifelong, monogamous marriage covenant between one man and one woman as the vessel to contain, nourish, and express it.

When the body makes intimate physical contact, the brain floods the system with dopamine. The dopamine forges a neural pathway to which the body is inclined to return. But the brain also produces oxytocin and vasopressin—a neurological bonding experience. God has hardwired the human being for more than pleasure during sex, but for intimacy and fidelity also. Thus, to defy the master is to defy God's design for human flourishing.

To experience the biological tick of sexual attraction is no more sinful than hunger or thirst. But desire, if nourished and indulged, drags the one who indulges it away and to death. This is the man who leans into the current of attraction, who allows the observation of beauty to become the long stare, who makes the woman he ogles into an object for consumption—as if she existed only to accommodate the shape of his appetites, as if she were a thing to be possessed, kindling to burn on the altar of his assumed power. Like the one who burns with anger. Like the one who kills. Like the fool.

IV. WHEN TO GOUGE YOUR EYE OUT

Two thousand years after the master's warning, children, adolescents, and adults became enclosed on all sides by electric sex emanating from televisions, touchscreens, and billboards. We became statistics, terraformed by hell to not only permit the objectification and abuse of human beings made in God's image but to indulge it. To celebrate it. To fund it with clicks and views and digital ideologies.

If the long, lecherous stare entices you to the degree that you stumble along the road of your apprenticeship to the master, do not take cautious, gradual action. Be swift and surgical. There are to be no bandages, only amputations. Let the reckoning be fast and brutal. Press the blade into the tear duct, past the soft tissue, and into the gristle, wedge the blade, and turn the lever until the eyeball pops free of its wet casing and hangs visionless from the socket. The offending eye—the eye of the long, lecherous stare—will lead the entire body into hellfire and destruction, so gouge it out. Throw it away. Suffer this slight loss and save yourself from utter destruction. The man who objectifies a woman will be held responsible. The problem is neither the woman nor her body—God created both good. The man who reduces a woman to an object chooses his evil, and it is his own evil for which he will answer before God.

If your hand reaches out to take hold of that which does not belong to you—to do harm to another with your wrenching, grasping, scraping, covetous clutch—then bury the axe in the wrist again and again until the body is free of the evil hand.

If you see a child standing motionless before a barreling locomotive, it is appropriate to tackle them out of harm's way. The child will likely be injured by the rescue but escape total annihilation. Escaping total annihilation is better.

The apprentice of Jesus must daily rule the body in submission to the master and his teachings. If your eye goes on looking, objectifying, gouge it out. Destroy the device, the vulnerability, the objects and scenarios that steward sin. Better to suffer these little deaths now than total death in the age to come.

V. SACRED FIDELITY

THE LIFELONG, MONOGAMOUS marriage covenant between one man and one woman is not only the sole vessel strong enough to contain the wild power of human sexuality; it is also a sacred, God-given pairing that, rightly realized, can reflect the union of Jesus and his people. No one is required to marry, and no one is more valuable or more realized in their humanity for marrying. God will invite many to emulate Jesus specifically in the sacred call to singleness, chastity, and celibacy. But for those who marry, the covenant must be honored with fidelity.

Four times in the ancient Hebrew Scriptures, the God of Israel makes promises to his people and asks, in return, for their faithfulness. The covenant is not a contract—you do your part to make me happy, and if you fail, I am no longer obligated to uphold my end of the bargain. God's covenantal love is unconditional. Even though humanity will fail to uphold their end of the covenant, God will remain faithful.

In centuries past and in civilizations abroad, men banished their wives for unfaithfulness, for burning dinner, for failure to bend to their control, or for "better" options. Still today, many men and women enter the sanctity of marriage with all the careful foresight and judiciousness with which they might select a TV miniseries or a microwaveable dinner. Along the road of shared life, they confront the inevitability of conflict, of incompatibilities. A void yawns open between them, swallowing up their will to love. They divorce. But the covenant yet binds them. When a man who has dismissed his wife in divorce goes looking for the embrace of another woman, he victimizes the wife he put out with adultery.

Any and every person who invites the wild passion and braves the rattling gales of marriage must take seriously Jesus' invitation to die. The husband and wife must each look to the other and say, again and again, throughout the years, I am prepared to lay myself bare to love you. I will fail you, and you will fail me. Will you walk with me anyway?

Even so, the covenant can be broken, and the married person can be released by God. Sexual betrayal can break the covenant. Abuse and abandonment can break the covenant. The breaking of the covenant is a terrible seriousness with devastating long-term consequences and should be engaged and addressed with sober sincerity and tender compassion. Marriage is among the most misunderstood and painfully misrepresented premises in a culture prone to its belittling. We like hyperbole to describe marriage, depicting it as either endlessly beautiful or desperately ugly.

The truth is that marriage is often beautiful, can be ugly, and is often very ordinary. Marriage can be difficult, and it can be pretty easy, and often is neither. It won't save your life, and it doesn't have to ruin it. Marriage is a micro-community of the most intimate kind: a man and a woman who consciously pledge to share their lives, serving and sacrificing for one another in the process.

The erosion and destruction of the covenant is not a sin insurmountable by the redemptive work of Jesus, but those who have endured its decline know that it is a devastating catastrophe. Ours is a world unkind and unaccommodating to sacred fidelity. If the temporal satisfaction of the individual is, as we are often led to believe, the highest order of human existence, the human condition is a sick, sad state of affairs indeed. But to serve and sacrifice for the sake of another is to emulate the master, is to emulate God. To emulate God is to experience and participate in the love of God, and the love of God cannot be broken.

VI. REJECTING ALL OATHS

THERE IS NO WORD spoken that escapes the ears of God. The integrity of human words is so enfeebled by our propensity to do other than what we say we will do that human beings reach for verbal reinforcements to boost and bolster the seriousness of their otherwise flippant decrees. I promise. I swear. I swear to God. And if a certain divine intimidation daunts us, we swear on our wallets, our lives, on our mother's grave. But all we have already belongs to God. Our lives were given to us by God. The grave will not be undone by our swearing but by God. No swearing can be whispered beyond the earshot of God, and the swearing itself serves only to reiterate the otherwise gossamer-thin, untrustworthy substance of our words.

But the truth is a thing of real solidity. The truth is confident, secure. The truth is in want of no bolstering, no trickery, no manipulation. Bolstering, trickery, and manipulation belong to the evil one; that they exist at all is indicative of a world without honesty and integrity. When the truth reigns in our words and in our deeds, swearing becomes suddenly and entirely worthless.

Let all your words, then, be nothing but truth.

Careless speech—the kind that creates the need for oaths—erodes trust and dismantles community. But the truth does more than *enforce* community; it *creates* community.

Thus, the master has forbidden oaths. First, legally binding oaths. The master himself refused to swear an oath to the living God when on trial before religious leaders. The master's earliest followers intentionally subverted the religio-political oath of their time and place, "Caesar is lord," with the refutation proclamation, "Jesus is lord. I do not pledge allegiance to Caesar. I pledge allegiance to Jesus." They would not take military oaths nor participate in warfare of any kind. The command of Jesus politicizes. It requires the disciple to live in constant questioning tension with the state.

But the master has also forbidden private oaths. The private oath is the verbal duct tape to bind the crumbling reliability of the one who swears it. Simple words with no integrity require reinforcement. The oath itself is not a strange, arbitrary evil, but that it exists and that we reach for it betrays our common, socially acceptable dishonesty. We do other than we say we will do. Not so for those who belong to the master. If we say we will do it, it will be done. If we say we will be there, no further goading or reassurance is necessary. The total weight of commitment and clarity is imbued in the single-syllable clarity of *yes* and *no*.

We will reorder and rearrange our lives to become a people who habitually honor our *yes* and sit comfortably and at peace within our *no*. The incredible, stark severity of the master's teaching demands solemn, spiritual consideration. We must become a people of the truth even in our most common utterances. All inconsistencies of speech and commitment, all failures of integrity belong to the evil one, the father of lies. There is no truth in him, so there must be no truthlessness in us. Let the pagans doctor their sickly pledge with promises, and let the Christian say only "yes" or "no" with more reliable solidity than a thousand oaths.

VII. LEX GRATIA

YOUR SANDALED FEET CRUNCH the pebbles and dust as you walk the roads of Galilee, the bright eastern sun bearing down overhead. You walk, always carrying a profound love for this land and its stories—the stories of your people. Your stories are the stories of Abraham, of Moses, of Israelite women walking dry ground through a parted sea, of old widows redeemed. Your stories are of warriors like Joshua and David. Your hope is Messiah, his sword raised, the blade bisecting the sun, who will one day come to lead his warriors triumphant, spill the blood of the oppressor, set your people free. Yours are the Psalms, the Prophets, the wisdom of Solomon. Your way of life is God's wisdom written on stone; God's story revealed in the Torah, God's law. But also in the Nevi'im, God's prophets and history. And in the Ketuvim, God's poetry and wisdom. The Scriptures.

The land you know is home to the same mountains and valleys and rivers of which your ancestors wrote in those ancient stories, reaching all the way back to "in the beginning." Your world is not a distant planet far removed from the ancients and their stories, but the land where those stories came to pass.

All is not well in the land of your heritage, of your people. After all, God chose Israel—your people—to become the means through which he would set the world to rights. But Israel failed, again and again, until her sin was so great that God allowed her to suffer the consequences of her evil: Babylon invaded the land, conquered its people, and drove them from their home. Decades later, your people are back in their ancestral home, but the land still belongs to pagans. Your home, the city of Capernaum, is a militarized zone occupied by a foreign presence for some seventy years. Though the land belongs to your ancestors, it is ruled by the Roman Empire.

These great centurion bullies remind you of their lumbering presence constantly. They make daily security rounds down the city borders. Your uncle, a farmer, was so burdened by Roman taxes he was forced to sell his fields and work as a debt-slave on the ground that once belonged to his father and his father before him. These occupying powers care nothing for your stories, your way of life, or your God. They know nothing of Israelites walking dry ground between a parted sea. They use their high position to abuse your people daily through political, mental, emotional, and physical means.

With these stories and centurions never far from your waking world, you rise and set off into your village to prepare for a day's work of fishing. Dawn is breaking in the east; the air is cool and damp. As the homes around you wake and stir, you catch wind of conversations among rousing villagers. There is a sense of excitement in a nearby dialogue. Curious, you move toward the voices. They are discussing a traveling stranger. A rabbi. A prophet. He's been moving throughout the region, preaching, healing the sick, casting out demons. Crowds have begun to flock to him. He's already gathering apprentices. He's called Jesus of Nazareth. You set out to join the crowds clamoring for an earful of what this enigmatic and alluring teacher might have to say. With hundreds of people, young and old, surrounding him on all sides, Jesus from Nazareth begins to unpack his manifesto on life in what he calls the kingdom of God.

You didn't know then that decades later, those same apprentices of Jesus from Nazareth would remember those words and that manifesto as they were tied to stakes, looking down at the emperor's servants as these henchmen touched their torches to the pyre just before these disciples of Jesus were consumed in flame.

That's how it might have been some two thousand years ago. But go somewhere else for a moment. Maybe there, you're looking out a window on the French countryside in the early 1940s. Rumors of the occupying German army's barbaric violence and genocide continue to reach your village. Talk of ovens and gas chambers and the cold, systematic execution of terrified children. You step outside your cottage one grey, foggy morning, anxious, a tremble in your breath, with an open and weathered copy of the Scriptures.

Or maybe it's much later than that, and you're a terrified Syrian caught in the endless storm of civil war—the crushing reality of encroaching violence closing in on you and your family day after day after day. You gather with other Christians in secret, and you open the Bible to read what Jesus from Nazareth says is best.

Or maybe it's now and you're you. And you look up from the book in your hands. The world you know is shrinking all the time via media access and globalization, a never-ending parade of paranoia and sociopolitical vitriol. Suicide bombers, police brutality, immolations, cars purposefully steered into helpless pedestrians, ongoing executions, near-daily mass shootings. The fresh and baffling threat of nuclear war, as if no one has learned anything in eight decades. North Korea could aim missiles at Guam. Whoever runs your country could retaliate. Down the street, domestic abuse. Child abuse. Stabbings. Beatings. Animal cruelty.

Against the terrible backdrop of reality, the book in your hands—this one—is about to talk about what Jesus from Nazareth says is best.

Before recorded history, the devil was flung from heaven to strike the world like a meteor, out of which boiled contaminating sewage. Before recorded history, the devil was violent. A murderer. The first story beyond the goodness of God's garden in the beginning is of one brother killing another. Violence is like that: a terrible contagion. Violence accomplishes little beyond destruction and self-replication. It destroys, then echoes, like a consuming fire ravaging dry woodland. The devil—the Satan—drags himself to and fro in a world of tinder.

Once, long ago, God's wisdom on stone came to a violent people to curb the escalation of violence, to quell bloodlust with limitations: to protect his people, God fenced them in. The fence was not what God nor his people envisioned for their flourishing but became necessary to protect them from death. Repay violence in turn but do no more. Ten times it repeats throughout the Hebrew Scriptures: an eye for an eye, but no more. *Lex talionis.* The law of retribution. Equal to, but never more than the injury—curb violence and thwart the inevitable snowball of proliferating vengeance.

Children require this restriction, as do men and women and entire nations. The law of God on stone is forward-thinking as a stricture for unbridled retribution. Jesus knew this well when he reached deep into the heart of these commands to draw out the stark and terrifying heartbeat within them. God's wisdom on stone called for God's people to love others as they love themselves. Lex talionis was mere concession. In Jesus' revolutionary teaching, God has not suddenly changed. The will of God has always been gracious and forgiving love that does more than limit violence. It puts the cycle of violence to an end by absorbing it and silencing its echo. Do not take an eye for an eye. Show mercy.

In the social and moral economy of God's kingdom, the fire of violence is no longer merely fenced in; it is quenched outright by those made brave in love. The community of Jesus, no longer bound by any vows nor by political or national ties—those who have severed all allegiances to other kings and other kingdoms and who refuse to objectify others—will not go to war with the enemy or against the enemy. They won't go to war at all.

They will not take revenge. They will not retaliate. They will not use violence, not even to resist violence. For what good can there be in using evil to repay evil? This violence-quenching way of life is anything but passive. A passive party would be consumed by the fire of violence and be brought to an end, but the person of active love absorbs the fire of violence so that violence itself is brought to an end. Evil meets an unmovable object, willing to be consumed to quench violence rather than becoming a combustible agent that gives violence life.

Listen! You apprentices of the master. No evil person or outsider is to be met with violence. Do not use violence to resist evil. Violence seeks to destroy the other. To overpower their consent.

To violate their intrinsic God-given value with brute force. Do not use violence to resist evil. Do not take revenge.

Instead, violence must be swallowed up and made no more by the terrible beauty of self-sacrificial love. As Jesus endured the cross for his enemies, so too his apprentices reject the way of the devil and do no violence, not even against enemies that seek to destroy us.

Your sandaled feet crunch the pebbles and dust as you walk the roads of Galilee, the bright eastern sun bearing down overhead. A road you walk daily in the realm of the oppressor. But Jesus from Nazareth calls out over the crowds. His command is as provocative as it is incredible: Do good to the enemy. In suffering insult and injury, do good to them. In being abused and oppressed, do good to them. In being made to give part of what is yours to the enemy, give even more. Self-sacrificial love is not passive but an active way of life. This is what God is like.

In the most egregious of violent insults, do not nurture the cycle of violence. Refuse it. Do this as Jesus did. Demonstrate a radical willingness to sacrifice, even for enemies, even at the expense of oneself and of social norms. Refuse the way of the world handed down across millennia of violence and entitlement, of governments and powers. Let grace and compassion that the world does not understand become the law. This is what God is like.

Lex gratia. The law of grace.

Lex gratia is neither passivity nor retribution, but a third way. The way of the master defies the unthinking fundamentalism that can conceive only of violence or passivity rather than a creative mercy, empowered by the Spirit of God within the master's apprentices. The third way transforms violence and hatred into peace. Blessed are the peacemakers.

To make peace is often impractical in the minds of those who do not follow the master. For them, a world without regrettable but necessary violence and self-defense, without weapons and warfare, is too strange a reality to imagine, let alone create. But lex gratia is not about practicality or self-preservation or even social order. It is about the love of the master for all people—including enemies—made manifest in his apprentices. For this, they must, as in all things, take up their crosses and follow him.

Because the master requires more than simply abstaining from violence against enemies, he commands that his apprentices love their enemies. For the master, it is not enough to love and care for those connected by blood, or tradition, or proximity, or interests. Anyone can do that. Most people do.

We often believe—consciously or subconsciously—that we are within our rights to love some and not others. But the master understands all human beings—in all their shaking, shivering configurations of awfulness—as yet made in the image of God himself and loved by him. We are to be like God. Your enemies—be they personal, national, or abstract—are loved by God and therefore must be loved by you. This is what God is like. Be like God, who is whole, mature, complete.

The Galilean villager who has known life only under the oppressor. The apprentice tied to the stake. The apostle hung upside down on a cross, like his master. The French civilian in enemy-occupied territory. The terrified Syrian surviving civil war. The harried reader, ever fretful of tyranny and nuclear bombs. The master's words ring out across centuries and civilizations, unchanging: Do not repay evil with evil. Love your enemies.

Lex gratia. The law of grace.

VIII. SECRET GOOD

YOU MUST DISTRIBUTE MERCY, compassion, and justice to the so-called worthless person. There are right and wrong ways to live, and the way of mercy is right. You must willingly sacrifice time, energy, and finances to close the gap of need that yawns open in the lives of those the rest of the world has forgotten, because God remembers them, and you, apprentice to the master, represent God on earth. To become the type of person capable of such good requires proximity to the master. Proximity to the master's teaching and presence reshapes the soul. The soul reshaped will propel its pilot to love God and other people as God loves them.

Love is never performative. Do not be like an actor on a stage who makes a great show of all the good he or she does. Such an actor is not you, really, but a mask, an affectation, a character.

God cannot stare knowingly into the soul of this character because this character is a fiction. But when the apprentice does good with no stage, no megaphone, no choreography, the good they do goes unseen by much of the world but remains ever before God in all its naked, brilliant glory. God sees the secret good and the one who does it.

So go and do good. Distribute mercy. But do so with no intention of being seen or lauded or loved by anyone other than God.

A hidden life is strange to most of us. In the world we know, life unfolds on glowing glass surfaces and in the public square. The world, as we know it, is constantly logged by photographs with tidy, posturing captions, by the constant connectivity of digital data, GPS, messages sent and received through space in an instant. A hidden life—secret good—is as unfamiliar to us as good that never happened at all. Documented and broadcast good, we believe, is most real, is best. But performative good cannot permeate the true self because it is carried out by the false self. It funnels backward into the person of self-focus, into the ego.

Secret good seeks no audience nor any purpose other than good for goodness's sake. It searches out no platform but looks only to another for whom the good can benefit, even at the expense of the one doing it. Because the doer of secret good wears no mask, no costume, because they curate no veneer around the good they do, God sees it clearly. Beautifully.

Doesn't a good father greet his happy children? Doesn't he take them up in his arms and hold them? Doesn't a good father delight, without pretense or apology, at the indecipherable crayon scrawling that his children promise is his portrait? And doesn't a good father watch with eager eyes as his children—though they falter and fall—set to work doing good for no reason other than that he might see the good they do and the good in them that drives it? The good father requires no deeds of his children at all to love them, but because he loves them and loves others, he appoints them to good deeds.

Our good Father loves us as we spill, always spilling, into a world of the broadcast self. I did good things. Look at them all. I knew and said important things. I took lovely trips and arranged my lovely family before my camera's eager eye. I thought and said all the right, true, good things about art and politics and race and war. I wrapped myself in flattering garments, and the world saw me do it. I ate colorful dishes and demonstrated inspiring ideas and routines. I fasted from sugar. I saw the world. I bought things. I got here first. I was here. I mattered. Can you see me?

But the Father cannot see the spiraling, scraping actor—this bending cartoon character—because the character isn't real. Not there at all.

PARABLE: THE BEST YEAR

IT WAS THE BEST year by far for the partners and shareholders and for me. I opened new accounts to accommodate all the money; more than I could spend, probably. At this point, my money was making money, so I removed myself from day-to-day operations and bought property in Bermuda. All my life, I'd worked for a way out of the white-collar rat race, for freedom, and I'd finally pulled it off.

The vultures came pecking, of course. Coworkers rattling on about nonprofits and clean water and hurricane relief. A friend of mine, he donated to the local ballet academy, and they engraved his name into a little tile on the wall. When I asked him about it, he only shrugged. "It's tax-deductible," he said.

"Really?" I asked him. "The ballet?"

He looked away, already thinking about something else. "I think so," he said.

People were talking about how much money is a lot of money, but, really, it's all relative. I figured this is enough money for me to finally take it easy for once. Is that "a lot" or just enough? I figured I earned it, didn't I? If that's how much money it is, then that's how much money it is. It's a little or a lot, depending on who you ask. Someone else always has more anyway. That's the kind of thing I was thinking about the night before what was supposed to be my first flight east over the Atlantic to an island I'd never actually seen. My assistant had been the one to finalize the purchase, and she'd sent people to prepare the spot. One less thing for me to worry about. I'd earned it.

I was thinking about how much work I'd done to get to that point, about my money making money, about how soon I'd be pulling corporate strings from a lawn chair on a beach looking out on a turquoise sea. As soon as tomorrow and for the rest of my life. Then I was in the moment again, squinting down a busy highway through a rain-streaked windshield between bursts of frantic wiper blades. Then I was slipping—the whole car sliding—and my mind was processing the bleary yellow globes of oncoming headlights, awareness becoming horror. Then, the impact. Then I wasn't thinking anything at all.

IX. HOW TO PRAY

THE ACTORS PRAY as if on a stage—to be seen and heard and admired by an audience. These elaborate "prayer" performances are every bit as intimate and interpersonal as the cacophony of a mob. God cannot receive the prayer with sincerity because there is no sincerity in it. And the actors cannot know the God they petition in the public square because they ignore him in the quiet. Do not be like them.

And do not pray like those who belong to other gods, who go fretting and flailing and stacking up incantations and mantras and little dances in an effort to summon some otherwise indifferent deity, a chakra, a good vibe. Your Father in heaven knows you completely. He is completely aware of everything you need. God invites prayer, not for want of wish lists but for the sake of intimacy. Those who belong to other gods pray to genies, abstract energies, fictional characters, and demons. Do not be like them.

Yes, pray in public—the master did so—but not for acclaim. Yes, pray with others—the master did so—but not for their approval. Yes, pray at length—the master did so—but do not assume God requires a quota of words before he turns his listening ear to your prayer. Yes, pray repetitious or persistent prayers—the master did both—but do not assume God will only listen if you repeat yourself.

Pray like this:

> *God, you are not aloof or uncaring; you are my good*
> *   and loving Father.*
> *You are not distant; you are with me, all around me,*
> *   as close as the air in my lungs.*
> *You are beautiful and wonderful. Everything about*
> *   you is good.*
> *But our world is broken, and so are we. Make things*
> *   the way they should be.*
> *I need you. Take care of me today.*
> *Where I have failed, forgive me.*
> *Where others have failed me, teach me to forgive them.*
> *Lead me away from anything that might distract me*
> *   from you.*
> *Rescue me from the devil and his traps.*

X. A HUNGER ARTIST

THE WAY OF THE master is, like all committed lifestyles, a way of dedications and disciplines. To train in the ways of the master is to learn when it is appropriate and best to deny the base appetites of the body and mind in service to spiritual formation. Boxers and students of kung fu do this. Marathon runners and ballet dancers do this. Painters, academics, pianists, and plumbers do this. The primal and unsophisticated mind rings the bell of simple hungers, and the person of discipline must choose when to answer or else ignore the ringing bell in advance dedication to the person they are becoming: a champion, a master, an expert.

Like the ancients, apprentices of the master will fast. They will go without food and water for set and specific periods of time to focus the appetite on prayer, to respond to significant events, to stand with those who are hungry, to repent, or to rewire the appetites altogether. The apprentice is not an immaterial soul piloting a material form. The apprentice is neither a mere bag of blood and bone nor a spectral spirit. The apprentice is both body and soul. Fasting enables the body to see as the soul sees. When the apprentice enters into the time of fasting (or of any discipline that challenges or pains the appetites), they must not become like the actors.

The actors cinch themselves up and draw long, harrowing frowns down their sad, sagging faces. They speak often of the terrible discomfort they suffer in service to the towering majesty of their discipline. Oh, they say, how hungry I have become from all my fasting! Oh, they lament, how ragged is my voice from my many hours of prayer! The actors hand over both the work and the result of spiritual discipline to an audience. They build a fabricated holiness from the stacked plastic tokens of their audience's admiration. God does not know that character because that character is a fiction.

With all their pseudo-spiritual pyrotechnics, the actor makes their spiritual discipline a manipulation. They manipulate the reactions of their observers, and they attempt to manipulate God with the great spiritual razzle-dazzle of their effort. But discipline, for the apprentice, is not effort for effort's sake; it is a means to an end. The end is to know the master, to be like him, to become more and more over time the kind of person who lives in and operates out of the master's great love.

The apprentice must embrace the life of discipline, like the boxer, the student of kung fu, the marathon runner, the ballet dancer, painter, academic, pianist, and plumber. For the master's apprentice, discipline is never carried out to be seen, or recognized, or admired by other people. Discipline is only a vessel the apprentice boards and navigates into the fire of God's love. For them, the victory, the symphony, the finished painting, the dance is the love of God.

XI. YOUR TREASURE IS DOOMED

OUR TREASURES ARE THE things we cling to because of the value we assign them. Small children who cannot fathom wealth store up treasures for themselves. Given time, children become adults, and their treasure becomes their money. Adults amass treasures; the rich and powerful pile them up, display them, stockade them on all sides to push back the terrible inevitability of their loss. But they'll be taken anyway. One way or another, your treasure is doomed.

Your trinkets, toys, and riches will rust, rot, be scrabbled and chewed by vermin, pilfered by thieves, destroyed by time and misfortune. Only the love of God and the goodness of the master's way of life are eternal and invincible. There are only two ways to steward and spend your money: in ways that demonstrate your love for God and others, and in ways that do not.

The apprentice's handling of money will exemplify their love. How one spends their money demonstrates their character—reveals what matters to them most. If you want to know what a person does and does not love, check their bank statement.

But most of us, we like to think of ourselves as poor, or at least not so rich, because how can a poor person be held accountable for their spending? The upper class crane their necks upward to behold the superrich, several rungs up the economic ladder, and say to themselves, "I am not like them!" The middle class beneath them thinks the same, as does the lower class another step down. When one billion people worldwide live on less than one dollar a day, someone is always richer than you.

Throughout the Scriptures, financial and material wealth are consistently depicted as an affliction—a near-insurmountable obstacle to entering the kingdom of God. The master's apprentice practices financial divestment for the sake of the poor and for the sake of saving their soul from the entangling tentacles of wealth.

Though the master's apprentices may technically earn money and own possessions, neither belong to them. All the apprentice has and is belongs to God, who directs the apprentice's spending, saving, and giving. Because God is self-sacrificial love, he will never direct the apprentice to hoard their riches nor to concentrate their spending on themselves. Temporal riches, God knows, will rust and rot, but to repurpose the potentially contaminating power of wealth into a tool used to manifest the self-sacrificial love of God—such a thing lasts throughout this present age and into the age to come.

The master said that it is better to give than to receive, but most of the time we don't believe him. Not really, anyway. On paper, sure, it seems simple enough, but in practice, we think it would be much better to receive. We worry that the master's teaching was romantic idealism, impractical, dangerous. We fret that if we were to live as though these words were true, there would be nothing left for us, and without money and stuff, how can we be happy and safe and sound? All around us, the world takes us by the wrist, leans in close, hot, stinking breath in our faces, whispering—as the snake did in the garden—Don't believe God! Surely, at least on this minor issue, he was mistaken. Don't you deserve what you earn? And aren't you entitled to spend your money as you see fit? To enjoy your possessions as you would like? If the poor require money, let them earn it! But the master's words cut like a sword through the devil's lies: Giving is better than receiving. There is no partisan political system at stake, no worldly practicality to preserve, no loopholes, and no excuses. It is simply better to give than to receive. And in the ultimate demonstration of these words and their truth, the master, Jesus, set the example by giving his life away.

If the apprentice can learn to entrust their understanding of riches to God, they will be released to follow the master freely and enjoy the life he gives now and in the age to come. If the apprentice will not lay their wallets and bank accounts at the feet of Jesus, they will be filled with a terminal pollutant that will eclipse and, ultimately, snuff out the light within them. In the end, one's allegiance can be given to only one master: God or money. Choose this day whom you will serve.

XII. THE END OF WORRY

WHEN OUR ALLEGIANCES TO money and possessions are no more, when we have learned the art of generosity and the secret joy of doing good for good's sake, worry will be no more.

We dedicate our worry to that which preoccupies our hearts and minds, for we cannot fret over things of no consequence. We worry about money because we believe it is necessary for our happiness and well-being. We worry for our reputations and securities and comforts, and we can't seem to convince ourselves by way of information or volition that our reputation is sealed in God's favor, that our security in him is unshakeable, that his love is the greatest comfort of all. Maybe we know some of these things intellectually, but we don't know how to experience them.

Because worrilessness cannot be transmitted via information or willed into existence. Worrilessness is grown from the experience of practice. Birds do not worry for their status or provision. Flowers do not become anxious for their colors or blossoms. They are both, like us, subject to the sequence of time and chaotic unpredictability of life. But they are both, like us, known by God.

Worry only infects, corrodes, and cripples. It spawns on the damp basement floor of want and succeeds only in creating more want and more fear that this want will go unsatisfied. For so many millennia, the primitive (and then slightly less primitive) human beings that peered into the canopy of space overhead, reaching into it with their souls full of longing, have heaped up on their backs burdens of want they did not know were long ago satisfied by the God of love.

And those far from God remain unconvinced. They sit atop their hordes of riches accumulated by selfishness and injustice, terrified it will be taken from them, that it isn't enough. Those who live to eat and drink and dress can only scramble after these sad, empty things, all of which can and will be taken from them. They are right to worry. Do not be like them. Preoccupy yourself with the master's teaching, for the master's teaching is freedom.

But freedom does not negate suffering. Suffering will search for and find any and all who walk the often-unforgiving road of life in a broken world. Freedom is the hope of enduring suffering without being destroyed. Freedom is a hope that suffering cannot erase. Each day has its own troubles, but students of the master can learn to navigate and endure these troubles without being undone by them or the worry these troubles carry like parasites as they pass.

God enters into no contractual agreement with the well-behaved. He does not promise a life without suffering as a reward for obedience, and he does not impose suffering as punishment for those who fail. Failure and suffering are inevitabilities. But no failure and no suffering have the power to penetrate the majesty and invincibility of God's perfect love. I am still made in God's image. I am still God's child. I am still known and loved by God. And God will make everything new. Let tomorrow worry about itself.

Then come and see for yourself. The more you give of yourself, the more you empty yourself, the more the snake's constricting grip of worry loosens from around your neck. The more you give, the more you taste and see the goodness of giving and the futility of fear. If God knows us, loves us, has saved us, is saving us, *will* save us, if God's ultimate victory over suffering, sin, and death is secured even now, what is there, ultimately, to fear? What, then, deserves our worry?

Each of us must care, even for the little things of life. We care about ourselves, our loved ones, whether they have food and shelter. We care for our hopes and dreams, our futures, our simple joy and satisfaction. And we are not alone in our caring. God also cares for our needs, our wants, our simple desires. We bring our cares to him. Our hopes to him. Our desires to him. We bring him medical diagnoses and travel plans. We bring him job applications and student loans. We bring him mortgages and debt, hunger and thirst, want and need, and he cares for them as a loving parent cares for the safety, joy, and satisfaction of their child. Because he cares—because we are his—we don't have to worry.

An enemy pursued a man of God fleeing across a frozen lake. As the man of God ran, the ice shattered behind him, and his enemy sank. But the fleeing man went to his enemy, pulled him from the ice, and saved his enemy's life. The enemy then seized the fleeing man and jailed him, and he was executed the next day. The fleeing man trusted wholly in the power of love even in the face of death and was impervious to worry. Trouble still found him. But maybe, as the hangman fastened his noose, the fleeing man prayed, God, let my jailer be saved, that he, too, might be set free from worry. Amen.

XIII. EYE FULL OF SPLINTERS

WE CAN ONLY BE a people of reconciliation or a people of condemnation. Self-assessment is difficult for the human being—and a student of the master is no exception to this law of gravity. It is difficult for us to see ourselves not as our inflated sense of grandeur or hateful inner critic depicts us but as we truly are. Only God can see us for who we are without effort or obstruction, as broken and yet made beautiful by his love for us.

That we cannot see ourselves properly means our understanding of others is similarly faulty. We exaggerate their defects, accentuate their sparkle, or pile up our own shortcomings on their backs, unable to carry them ourselves. We become like a fool, a beam of tinder impaling us through the eye socket, calling out to someone else, You there! Don't you see there is a splinter in your eye? How shameful to go about with that splinter in your eye, we say, unable to lift our heads from the terrible weight of the wood beam that runs through our head, all but blinding us.

Aren't I like God, we say, in that I can see so clearly into someone else's inadequacies and blunders? That I distribute such mercy as to correct them? And thank God I was here to do it, we say, lest they wander the earth all their days with an eye full of splinters. Now, we say, if you'll excuse me, I need some rest. My head is heavy. Heavy is the head.

That person is like the actors. Like the phonies, the charlatans, the fakes. Do not be like them. Preoccupy yourself with the truth of your own condition: broken and beloved. By allowing ourselves an honest assessment of our own brokenness, God extends to us the precious gift of empathy. Empathy does not excuse nor permit evil but humanizes the evildoer as themselves, broken and beloved—like us. All the human family is bound by this sad unity of failure and the blessed gift of belovedness. When I commit myself wholly to the work of removing the beam of timber that impales me through the eye, I become sobered by my own great need for mercy and awed by God's willingness to distribute mercy as I need and more. The person changed by mercy becomes a vessel for mercy. Wounded by the beam that once ran through our head, our concern for splinters is humble. We become gentle. Here, we say, let me help you with that splinter. Believe me, we say, I've carried worse! Let me guide you to the one who removes splinters and beams.

And when we speak, some will yet be unprepared to hear us. When we give ourselves with gentle empathy, some will refuse to receive the gift of our wounded wisdom. For some who are far from God, the air between us and them will curdle our words, blacken them, and the gift of our humility will rebound from the calloused surface of their hardened hearts. So, the master's disciple must learn to embrace the terrible responsibility of correction without giving in to judgment. Judgment says, Oh, what a terrible failure you are, and oh, how clearly I, in all my righteousness, see you for the sinner you are. But correction says, This road leads to death; I know because I have walked it. Do not fail as I have failed. I care for you.

And when our care for fellow failures meets the inevitability of unprepared hearts, we concede our inability to coerce life and righteousness. We grieve that we will not be heard, not always, and we continue to walk the road of faithfulness anyway.

XIV. SNAKES AND STONES

KNOW THIS, SONS. KNOW this, daughters. When you speak, God listens. He cares. God needs no convincing, no qualifications: God, hear me because I am worthy. God, hear me because I have need. No, God wants to listen. God cares by default. Even a flawed father, on his best day, longs for the voice of his children. Toddlers do not consider that the reasons why their many requests may or may not be granted are numerous and complicated and beyond their understanding. But even a toddler can trust that their father loves them, listens to them, wants to hear from them. Even a toddler can assume that their father's general disposition is that of provision, generosity, an ear bent low to listen. Always listening. The good father does good to his children. The good father's innate character, his constant disposition, his set posture toward his children is blessing.

And yet, we are led astray by the illusion of self-sufficiency. We have become convinced by a lifestyle of digital accessibility and instant gratification that there's no pressing need to heap our thoughts and concerns into the lap of a father eager to receive them. We are led astray by the lie that he wouldn't care if we did. Not really. Hasn't he got better things to do than hear our petty Christmas lists? We are led astray by the lie that love means getting anything and everything we want, and when God, who loves us, will grant us no such destructive luxury, we take our business elsewhere. But God is not a storefront. God is not so simple and finite as to be made inaccessible by preoccupation. And God is not so foolish and permissive that he will accommodate the many ways we ask for death.

God is a good father. He welcomes us into his presence always, without performance or pretense, his arms open to us. Yes, come and ask! Even fathers of basic decency long for their children's voices, to grant their requests, to provide for them, to do more. God is much more than a father of basic decency. Come see. Ask.

XV. THE ENTIRE STORY IS THIS

ACROSS THE EPIC STORY of God—stories about temples and kings, about mountains and miracles, stories about parted seas and freed slaves—there are laws and commandments. Hundreds on top of hundreds doled out to ancient peoples and places in contexts and cultures long removed from the world of this book and you, the person holding it. These laws and commandments are not the story, but they are a part of the story—a story culminating in a day when the people of God are no longer begrudgingly fixed by statutes, but when they are made new by love and God writes his goodness on their hearts. If we were to summarize what lies at the center of these commands and this way of life, it would be this:

> **SO, IN EVERYTHING, DO TO**
> **OTHERS WHAT YOU WOULD**
> **HAVE THEM DO TO YOU.**

In the mundane things of life, in joy and tragedy, in our professional endeavors and in our homes, toward strangers and loved ones, toward friends and enemies, in all things, in all relationships, in everything we do. In everything and to everyone: do to others what you would have them do to you. Whatever it is that you wish others would do for you, do this for them. Actively. With initiative. This is the essence of all that is taught across the magnificent odyssey of the Scriptures. Add it up, and this is what you get. Love is the fulfillment of the law.

According to the master, it is not enough to reciprocate the good treatment of others and do no more. It is not enough to refrain from the kind of poor treatment you would not wish upon yourself. The law of love requires activity. The love of God is active. The love of God is not flimsy with sentiment, nor is it made ambiguous by the subjectivity of human emotion. The love of God is a radical and subversive way of life that challenges our assumptions of goodness and power. Imagine a way of life in which disciples of Jesus learn to live according to the story in summary.

It is a life in which husbands and wives value one another before themselves. A world in which parents, in the ongoing, stumbling struggle of raising children, constantly inconvenience themselves to remember what it takes to love their sons and daughters well, and pour themselves out to do it. Imagine a way of life in which gossip, slander, passive aggression, political acrimony, violence, xenophobia, racism, and sexism are all being stifled and snuffed out by disciples of Jesus who are learning to see all people as made in God's image, to walk in humility and empathy, to imagine new and creative ways to embody the truth of the master's teaching, and who disrupt their own comfort to do so. It begins with a question. In your every interaction, argument, interpersonal joy and frustration, ask, *If I were this person, with their story and their struggles and their wiring, how could someone reveal to me the subversive love of God?* Then do that. Then do it again.

XVI. THERE ARE ONLY TWO OPTIONS

WHAT WILL YOU DO with these stories and truths? Once, thousands of years ago in the ancient distance, a man stood on a mountain and brought forth the teaching of God himself. He set before the people two options: truth and lies. Life and death. The master is the final prophet. The final truth against which all other truth claims must be weighed and tested and judged.

There are many roads and many gates. Some roads and gates are wide enough to accommodate many people at once. If you were to move in concert with this lazy drift of life traffic, the road and the gate are wide enough, open enough to receive you.

And they lead off a cliff.

Other gates are smaller, set before narrow roads, and can be reached only by careful journey. To enter, one must do so thoughtfully and with intention. The small gate and the narrow road lead to life. Of those who hear the master's teaching, there are crowds, and then there are disciples. The crowds receive the master's teaching and think to themselves, *Interesting. Food for thought.* I like certain bits, they say, but others, not so much. They go on walking amongst the others, the current pulling them as they go, happy and adrift.

The disciple leaves the crowds. The disciple receives the master's teaching and is devastated and ruined and made new and changed. Though the master leads him to the narrow road, the disciple can go no other way, having seen the truth. The master himself is the gate by which the disciple enters the narrow road. And as we walk, he goes before us, beckoning us onward, enabling us to walk it at all.

There are only two options: the master or not.

The master is not a selection of intellectual propositions or philosophical suggestions. His person and his teaching are the only truth—the only way to God at all. The master beckons us to his gate and his road not as a summons to profit and prosperity but as an invitation to himself. Either we will say to the master, "Yes, I will live your way, with you," or else we say, "No, I will live my way, with me."

He is the decision we make again and again and again.

XVII. WOLF'S BLOOD

SEE THE WAY WOLVES gather about the tree trunks and bare their teeth, making a great show of their viciousness? But some wolves have learned to cover their fangs, fold themselves into convincing sheep-like shapes and disguises, and live amongst grass-eating lambs. And some point into the sheep pen saying, "See? These are sheep. They look like sheep. They bleat like sheep." Others disagree, saying, "Only God can say for sure whether or not they are sheep. It isn't my place." The master disagrees with them both.

Many have claimed and will claim to speak for God: leaders, visionaries, self-appointed prophets. Among them walk the sincere and the imposters. Here is how to identify them for who they truly are: watch to see if they obey the master's teaching and if their lives evidence the fruit of the master's way of life.

Are they people of blessing? Do they uphold the integrity of the Scriptures? Do they reject anger and animosity? When they fail, do they repent? Do they forgive, and do they seek forgiveness? Do they refuse to objectify others and honor other human beings as made in the image of God? Do they honor marriage covenants and reject political oaths? Are their words full of honor and integrity? Do they seek peace and refuse all violence? Do they practice righteousness for righteousness's sake rather than seeking approval and acclaim? Are they people of prayer, fasting, and spiritual discipline? Do they practice generosity and do they refuse the corrupting poison of wealth? Does their trust in God liberate them from fear and anxiety? Do they preoccupy themselves with addressing their own sin and spiritual formation before they correct others? Are they given over wholly to the all-encompassing allegiance and devotion to Jesus as lord and king, the only way to God?

Of course, no man and no woman will accomplish all these things without faltering, but look to those who claim to follow the master and ask, Are their lives evidence of these practices and dispositions? Imperfect though they may be, are they given over to the master's way of life and being changed by it? While the test of fruit is generally reliable, it is frustratingly complicated.

If the fruit is bad, the plant that bears it is likewise debased. Learn to see them for what they are. The test is not easy, not quick, not simple. Often, what appears to be bad fruit may prove to be an uncharacteristic and temporary failure, remedied by repentance and forgiveness. Sometimes, what appears to be a simple lapse in judgment is actually an indication of consistent unrepentant disobedience. The test cannot be completed in haste. We look not for perfection but for fruit. Beware the liars.

Many will stand before the master, having stuffed their lives full of forgery and deceit, and they'll wave their arms over long lists of religious accomplishments and spiritual spectacles, saying, "See? See all I have done?" But the master will ask, "Am I a list of goals to be achieved? Why didn't you come near to me and know me? If you knew me, you would be changed."

The will of God is more than an ethical category; it is the relational state of knowing and being known. A life dedicated to loving God and loving others will always be made manifest in inward disposition and evidenced by outward action, never one without the other. The love of God is not contingent on performance and good behavior, but the life of love is made manifest in what a person says and does—how they live because of what they believe.

Hearing this, the student looks within. "Wait," they ask the master, "is *my* life evidence of authentic discipleship?"

And the master replies: "Exactly the right question, my apprentice."

XVIII. THE END

IT IS NOT ENOUGH to hear the master's teachings, for them to mass into the imagination, little more than abstract strings of information. It is not enough to give them thoughtful consideration, not enough to assign them intellectual support. Now that you have received the master's teaching, put it into practice. Now that you have been given the master's commands, do them. Now that you understand the master's way of life, be obedient.

The one who puts the master's teaching into practice builds for themselves a house that can withstand the inevitable troubles of a broken world. The one who is obedient to the master will learn to become free from anger and lust. They will be peace-loving, gentle, compassionate, not anxious nor proud nor judgmental. They will be set free from the tyranny of fear, of greed, of materialism, of anxiety. Though they may know poverty and sickness, though they will stumble and fall, and though they will undoubtedly endure suffering, they will know the secret of hope.

The foolish person builds for themselves a house of sugar and straw. The storms of life topple and dissolve it, and the fool sits hopeless in the wreckage, exposed to the elements. When this chapter comes to an end, there will be only those who accept the master's teaching and those who reject it. To accept this teaching is to enter a lifetime of practice. Practice is not instant mastery; it is trial and error, success and failure, struggle and growth. The one who enters the life of practice will not do so alone; they will be empowered by the Spirit of God himself within them, and surrounded, bolstered, and at times carried outright by the family of God that is the church. We enter through the small gate and stay the narrow course, following the example of the master who goes before us.

He leads, we follow.

BOOK THREE: THE MANUAL OF DISCIPLINES

THE ARMAMENTARIUM

A NOTE FROM THE AUTHOR

I. – VIII. THE MASTER'S PRACTICES

IX. A BRIEF WORD ON THE END

FINAL NOTE FROM THE AUTHOR

DISCIPLE'S VOW

FINAL PARABLE

EPILOGUE

"I am afraid of pain and I suppose that is what we have to have to get grace. Give me the courage to stand the pain to get the grace, Oh Lord. Help me with this life that seems so treacherous, so disappointing."

FLANNERY O'CONNOR, *A Prayer Journal*

"I am a frayed and nibbled survivor in a fallen world, and I am getting along. I am aging and eaten and have done my share of eating too. I am not washed and beautiful, in control of a shining world in which everything fits, but instead am wondering awed about on a splintered wreck I've come to care for, whose gnawed trees breathe a delicate air, whose bloodied and scarred creatures are my dearest companions, and whose beauty bats and shines not in its imperfections but overwhelmingly in spite of them."

ANNIE DILLARD, *Pilgrim at Tinker Creek*

THE ARMAMENTARIUM

Holy Father,
Spread my arms upon the cross
That I might, in every moment, give myself away
As you do.
Make my cross into a spike
To drive through the skull of the evil one
That in my thoughts he would have no refuge
That in my deeds he would have no resource
That in my words he would have no voice.
Amen.

ON THE DISCIPLINE NECESSARY TO PLAY THE HARP

IF YOU'RE ANYTHING LIKE me, then you know about the occasional head injury. Maybe you've pressed a towel to your bleeding head in the darkened backseat of a fifteen-passenger van, the sky beyond your window a star-speckled canopy of velvety blue-black. Maybe you couldn't keep the pressure properly applied, bouncing around on the bench seat as the van capered over the craggy, pockmarked asphalt of another Corn Belt highway in America's rural Midwest.

When you spend months on the road, the days and weeks blur together. Where were you? Illinois? Indiana? Aren't there cornfields in Iowa? The headache wasn't helping.

You'd somehow struck yourself in the forehead with a microphone during the evening's performance. You don't plan injuries like these. They just sort of happen. You show up to another local dive, unload all your guitars and drums and amplifiers, a mess of wires and glowing tubes and circuit boards. You wait around all afternoon and evening, you play music for a little while, then you pack it all up and head for the next city.

But maybe you're also low on cash. Maybe you survive on a sum total of five dollars a day. No more, no less. So, maybe when your "salary" is a five-dollar per diem, you get creative. You learn things. Cheap pasta is a dollar a box. You can get a can of off-brand marinara for eighty-nine cents. You can survive for weeks on peanut butter sandwiches for mere nickels and dimes.

When surviving on five dollars a day, thirty-five dollars a week, for four to six weeks straight, you learn to bypass hotels. Someone will usually let you sleep on their floor if you ask nicely. You keep at it long enough, you learn a few things about sleeping on floors, like avoiding bachelor pads where food and space are likely in short supply. Big boarding houses rented by a dozen energetic twenty-somethings are a last resort. Sure, they may have video games and good attitudes, but the place will likely be a mess. It'll probably smell. Especially if the twenty-somethings are guys. The twenty-somethings will want to stay up all night, and you have to get to Iowa or Nebraska or wherever the heck you're going tomorrow. No, when panhandling for a free floor on which to sleep, you prioritize the suburban family home. You look for the "cool" parents who brought their kids and their kids' friends to the show. The forty-somethings in band T-shirts.

The suburban family home is clean. There's food there. The suburban family home has bedtimes, a spare room or two, air-conditioning. The suburban family home has paid their cable bill. When the excited twenty-somethings tell you about their "very cool" apartment and PlayStation 2, you say, "I'm not sure what our plan is just yet." You say, "That sounds great; I'll get back to you," and you keep looking for the suburban family home.

And maybe, if you're anything like me, it's the suburban family home to which you are en route as you watch the endless wallpaper of cornfields spool out in either direction from the van's window, pressing that towel against your forehead to stop the bleeding. When you arrive, the family leads you up the steps to the night's accommodations, and you go galumphing in, more than a half dozen of you, sweat-streaked and stinking, as another mom and dad offer a smiling tour of the guest rooms, saying, "Help yourself to whatever is in the fridge!" And you make with the pleasantries, you respectfully decline, "Oh, no thank you, you're too kind," wanting to be left alone with the cabinets, with the cereal and potato chips and Fruit Roll-Ups.

But maybe on this particular night, you step into the family room and stop. There, in the corner, across from the couch, stands a giant, golden harp. It must be six feet tall, a great shining column attached to a sliding arch fixed with strings so thick they catch the light. Enormous and imposing and alien. Maybe the only real-life harp you've ever seen. So, you ask, "What's with the harp?"

The parents suddenly beam, some secret knowledge passing between them as they summon their teenage daughter into the room. "She plays," they say. "Would you like to hear?"

You say that you would, assuming the young lady might protest, but she smiles and nods and moves with confidence to the instrument. She lifts her hands, and with a series of deft, elegant movements, she calls forth music from the harp, and it fills the suburban family home. Beautiful, otherworldly music. You sit there listening, pressing a fresh square of gauze against your forehead. The others, one by one, stumble into the living room and become similarly transfixed. It isn't the musicianship. You're all musicians. It isn't giftedness, per se. Would you even recognize a harp prodigy if you heard one? Some of your friends are incredibly gifted players. It isn't that. It's what all of you knew must have been the kind of lonely dedication necessary to actually get good at playing a harp. Anymore, who plays the harp?

And maybe many years after that night, you will be haunted by the sound of that harp without remembering its song. You won't remember that home, exactly, or the face of the young lady who played it, but you will remember the practiced precision with which she took to one string and then another, commanding melody from this ancient-looking golden monolith. You'll think, There was truth in the harp waiting to be summoned with only the flesh and bone of a player's fingers. Any player. But the harp will not yield mastery at the behest of my simple, inelegant want. I could sit there, and I could pluck at its strings. Maybe I could find an innocent, childlike melody in its curious apparatus, but I could not wield the instrument in such a way as to pour from it transfixing, ethereal song that would spill down over my lap and flood the living room of my suburban family home, traveling up the walls, cresting and colliding overhead, like a chorus of angels harmonizing their approval of great and glorious discipline.

I. PRAYER

THE EVENING IN MY home is a sacred space. My wife and I engage the simple domestic rituals of evening as if they were sacraments, beautifully routine and yet imbued with the presence of God. We prepare food for ourselves and our kids. The five of us gather in our kitchen, a kind of controlled chaos, and each of us brings the things of our own lives to set on the table—the day's events, the moment's thoughts. We offer these things up freely and without careful premeditation or censorship, these pieces of ourselves that, when shared, become the mortar of our souls' connections. One child spills his food. Another complains about the menu. Someone laughs. All of it belongs to the sacred space of evening.

We speak plainly, or with passion. We show affection or volunteer disagreement. We present to one another the fibers and filaments of our lives and personhood across the ordinary exchange of time and attention. As evening unfolds, my wife, known for her candidness and authenticity, walks comfortably in her fully realized self, completely vulnerable in love. Here, she is uninterested in cosmetics or formal fashion and expends no effort to configure her words with careful social sensitivity. My wife, who is her authentic self by day and by night, gives to me the entire truth of herself, laid bare by years of intimacy and a soul connection shared and enjoyed only by her and me.

All these things are what it means to pray.

Prayer is a life of evening intimacy. Sunday school graduates cannot help but hear the word *prayer* and imagine themselves, eyes squinted shut, palms pressed together, fingers skyward, reciting lists to an invisible cosmic Wizard of Oz. Prayer became for us a procedure to be accomplished, a list of requests that, if we didn't pray it, would remain forever beyond the scope of God's concern or good graces. The practice of prayer became a kind of spiritual treadmill to which one had to devote begrudging consistency for the sake of spiritual fitness.

But the true life of prayer is the ongoing art of divine intimacy and consistent, disciplined self-disclosure. Knowing us completely, the God of the universe wants intimacy, not information. God cannot be denied information, but intimacy is ours to extend or withhold. Intimacy cannot be manufactured by empty ritual, nor does it materialize only in the air of thoughtless spontaneity. Intimacy requires time, patience, and practice.

Intimacy necessitates the ordinary and unspectacular along with the crisis and the celebration. These are the hallmarks of the life of a praying person.

The time of prayer does not begin and end only in the quiet, the dark, in solitude. The time and place of prayer is in the dark and in the light, in the quiet and in the chaos, in the structured rhythms and interrupted routines of all life. Just as the bond between my wife and me was forged across years of private conversation and public laughter, in whispered confessions and in the ordinary prose of everyday dialogue. This profound familiarity was built in bedrooms and on beaches, across dinner tables and in traffic, on dates and on telephones, through letters and in knowing looks across crowded rooms.

And so, there are many ways to pray.

The first kind of prayer is conversational. During this kind of prayer, one brings thoughts, emotions, concerns, confessions, and requests to God, and that person, in turn, listens for God's response. In sharing, the praying person might speak aloud or in the quiet privacy of their mind. They might sit still or go on a walk. The goal of this practice is not completion, nor even being "answered," in any traditional sense. The goal is to know God and be known by him. When the praying person listens, they quiet their mind, limit their distractions, and they invite the Spirit of God in them to disclose what God is saying. God then uses his access to our thinking, feeling, and imaginations to create in our mind images, words and phrases, and emotional sensations. When we tell someone else what we hear, this is called *prophecy*.

Of course, our minds and feelings are imperfect and prone to wander, so there is no guarantee that what one experiences in the time of listening prayer is objectively and definitively from God, but the person who prays learns to ask, to wait, and to listen. What occurs in the space of listening, they believe, could be what God is saying. When a scene unfolds in their imagination, when a word suddenly springs to mind, they take hold of it and bring it into focus. They ask, "Is what I am hearing consistent with the Scriptures?" The Spirit might challenge their interpretation of the Scriptures, but he will not contradict its teaching. If what they hear stands in opposition to the written Word, it is not from God. If it is consistent with the truth of the text, they weigh it carefully. What does it mean? Where does it lead them? What does it mean to obey it? These are the components of conversational prayer.

Another kind of prayer is called contemplation.

There are moments in the evening when my son sidles up next to me. Maybe he sits with me while I talk to his mother or while the light of some movie flickers on his face, and we sit together in silent observance. As the distractions of life unfold around us, he gets closer to me, threads his small arms around mine, lays his head against my shoulder, my chest. If we sit together long enough, he might shift, resituate himself, and moments later, realizing he's drifted, turn to me to ensure my presence and come closer yet again.

This is the prayer of contemplation, in which there are no lists and no itinerary to speak of, only closeness, gazing, resting. During the time of contemplation, the praying person sets the attention of their mind, their heart, and their soul, as best as they know how, on God. They remind themselves of his nearness, of their desire for intimacy, and they thread their arms around his, lay their head on his shoulder, his chest. When they drift, they return to his side again and again. The prayer is a prayer of togetherness: closeness, gazing, resting.

Another kind of prayer is the prayer of intercession, during which one asks God to provide for their needs, grant them their desires, intervene in their lives and in the lives of others, and alter the reality of the world as they know it. Asking God for things is not the impersonal act of presenting a shopping list to a genie. The one who prays must remember always the configuration of a universe populated by autonomous beings. That each of us has been given a real say precludes any possibility of a timeline forever settled by God's unilateral control. Instead, God has handed over a certain amount of control to us, and while this ensures the wild and beautiful possibility of love, it also requires the inevitability that we can and will choose other than God. Even so, the God of relational love and eternal good voluntarily enters the bedlam of our evil and foolishness and—without compromising our freedom to choose—works for our good within it.

Having been entrusted with the truth of his goodness and faithfulness, yet aware of our own capacity to do evil, we may bring to God our wants and needs, confident of his willingness to care for us and of his power to do us good without being undone by the reality of a broken world in which not all prayers are answered. Intercession cannot be reduced to a simple exchange of requests and provisions, but together with all prayer, intercession contributes to the patchwork mural of relational love.

For me, the time of prayer grows from a bouquet of varied dispositions. The father of these dispositions is eagerness—a great, rollicking, childlike anticipation to set myself on fire with love and wonder. The bride of eagerness is need—the hunger and desperation that enable me to drag myself, tired and warbling, into the presence of he who holds and restores me, unshaken by whatever recent mud-sodden string of failures has soiled me. Eagerness and need bear troublesome children, and it is out of these dispositions that I also pray.

Their firstborn is duty, begrudgingly fulfilled, from which I will myself into the place of prayer, one foot before the other, as one carries themselves by the nape of their own neck to do exercise, algebra, or swallow cough syrup. The sibling of duty is emptiness—a state of being from which no real intimacy can be exchanged. But emptiness can be reshaped over time by consistency—an unwillingness to abandon the rhythm of prayer even when it feels voided by rote.

But the gnarled cousin of these siblings, scaly and stooped, is performance, which can accomplish no prayer at all. Performance is the spidery hobgoblin that covers my face with a mask, lays ribbons and capes on my back, effectively hiding me from sight altogether, silencing my voice until all that remains is a silent effigy no more capable of relationship than a wooden doll. Eagerness, need, duty, and even emptiness can all come before God in prayer, but the performer cannot pray because they do not exist. They are an affectation, a ruse. God cannot nurture intimacy between himself and the actor any more than he can accept confession from the whirring click-click-click of a windup toy.

The performer, only an actor, hides his gaze from God, peering out of his mask through black holes, no more feeling in them than a crab's eye at the end of a stalk.

II. MEDITATION LITERATURE

SOME STORIES NEVER END. They aren't intended to be read from cover to cover, concluded, and filed away in the annals of the intellectual mind. Some stories must be read and reread, backward and forward—selections, long stanzas, single phrases. Some stories must be examined and pondered from all angles, and, when lifted by the reader and rotated in the reader's grasp, each new season of life becomes a beam of light passing through the story's prism. To lift the story is to read it. To rotate the prism is to study it, consider it carefully, to meditate on it. Lift and rotate. Lift and rotate.

The ancient scrolls that together make up the library of writing we call the Bible—the Scriptures—are that story. Each word was selected and breathed out by the Spirit of God in collaborative concert with dozens of human authors across centuries and cultures, forms, and genres, capturing and immortalizing the story of God, humanity, and the universe. Because each word is God-breathed, the words and stories carry in them the authority of God. Every student of the master must learn this story again and again. Every student of the master must devote themselves wholly to a lifetime with meditation literature—writings divinely designed for reading and reflection, again and again and again.

The blood and guts and bones of this story—the absolute core truth of it all, about a loving God, his wayward lover, and the relentless redemption of all things through Jesus—are not hidden away from an ordinary reading of the text. They sit wonderfully on the surface of the page for readers young and old, simple and learned, wise and foolish. But the tendons and sinews that hold it together, the nerves and cartilage, the subatomic particles—all of them masterfully designed with detail and precision—require a lifetime of reading and can never be exhausted. Always lifting the prism high, always turning it in the light.

This epic body of work is too beautiful, too profound, too complex to bend to the whims and wishes of any individual reader. It has, and will always be, a work intended for the reading, interpretation, application, and formation of entire communities. You, student of the master, adopted into God's community, must submit your reading and understanding to the wisdom and discretion of your brothers and sisters. The family of God—priests and poets, scholars and laypeople, pastors and historians and linguists—have dedicated themselves to the ongoing work of reading, understanding, and applying the story for centuries. Any new insights must be weighed against the work and wisdom of those who came before us, and any reading that deviates from historic readings and applications handed down by the family of faith across generations must be approached with a careful, critical evaluation.

The Bible is confrontational and provocative. It can and will force every reader to grapple with the terrifying dissonance between what they believe to be true, what they want, and what God says is true, the life to which God calls them, and that which they must lay down (painfully, for now) in order to experience the freedom and joy appointed for them as the beloved (eternally). The reader must respect the story and its authors enough to reject the terrible impudence of reconfiguring their words to accommodate ever-evolving personal and cultural sensitivities.

Read, but do more than that. Reread. Meditate. Ponder. Study. Pore over the writings and seek out the wisdom of others who came before you, who read alongside you, who, like you, must dedicate their lives to knowing the writings well.

Lift and rotate. Lift and rotate.

III. VARIOUS DISCIPLINES FOR DYING

EVERYONE WHO BECOMES AN apprentice of the master must adopt a lifestyle of training. The way of the master is more ancient than kung fu, boxing, or ballet. It originates in God himself, who is before all things. The practices of discipleship are not performances nor demonstrations of good behavior to curry the favor of God, because God's favor is forever on us and cannot be bought by practice. The practices alone are not enough to effect real change but are empowered by the Spirit of God in us to make us more like Jesus. Practice, as with all ways of life, is how the disciple actualizes intellectual belief in outward action and, in doing so, is formed over time by the things they choose to think and say and do. In training, the bodybuilder becomes stronger, the gymnast more agile. An apprentice of Jesus, through practice and the power of the Spirit, becomes more like Jesus. The master's practices do not cultivate spiritual completion, because the master has already accomplished spiritual completion on the apprentice's behalf. Instead, the master's practices are appropriate means of responding to the love of God, and channels through which we experience intimacy. The practices do not make us smarter or better or more spiritual. They don't earn for us anything. They are means of redirecting our attention to the miracle of what we already have. Here are some ancient core practices and how to do them.

FASTING

During a fast, one deliberately abstains from food for a set period in order to discipline the spirit by disciplining the body. We put the body through a small trial in order to refine focus on and need for God, transform physical hunger into spiritual hunger, demonstrate solidarity with those in need, and respond to sacred or grievous moments in our lives and in the world.

A traditional fast begins at dawn and concludes at dusk, abstaining from breakfast and lunch. Within the empty space created by skipping these meals, the fasting person prays. Each time they become conscious of their desire for food, or experience any hunger pang, they utilize these bodily alarms as cues to pray—a monastery bell ringing within the body itself. The time of fasting prayer acknowledges hunger before God—that we are finite and needy, subject to impulse and appetite, and that the desire of our hearts is to be completely satisfied by him. We ask God to receive our hunger as prayer, to use it to teach and change us, and in asking, we acknowledge that we are embodied beings, body and soul.

When we fast to overcome temptation and sin, we spend the time of prayer in confession and repentance, using our bodily need for food to acknowledge our spiritual need for restoration. When we fast to stand in solidarity with the poor, we spend the time of prayer on their behalf, and we give the money and resources we would otherwise expend on our own appetites for their sake. When we fast as a response to sacred moments or in grief, we ask God to transform our physical hunger into a spiritual hunger for the renewal of all things. Fasting can be practiced in weekly, monthly, or quarterly rhythms. Because fasting is much more than the passive act of skipping a meal or two, a fast is not to be undertaken in haste. The apprentice chooses the rhythm, and prepares their heart, mind, and schedule to accommodate the fast.

WORSHIP

Affection changes those who give and receive it. When it is received rather than rejected or repurposed, affection humbles the recipient by gifting them the things they understand are all too often missing in the tragedy and chaos of a broken world: kindness, affirmation, and love. But the power of affection to reshape the soul is made manifest also in the one who gives it freely; affection changes the giver and the receiver. Like generosity of finances, or secret righteousness, or justice, the gift of affection draws the giver up and out of the mire of self-obsession that otherwise dominates the resting human disposition and imbues in them the power to become an agent of blessing.

But the exchange of affection between the human being and the God of the universe is a primordial cosmic exchange during which the veil between heaven and earth thins, becoming something more than expressed fondness; it is the emotional, spiritual, and physical demonstration of love and praise that we call worship.

Worship can be accomplished in prayer, with thoughts and words expressed to God acknowledging his beauty and goodness. It can be carried out with voices and musical instruments and arrangements or in writings and paintings. It can be practiced through the giving of finances or in acts of justice. These gestures are like a meal prepared for a friend, a gift given to a child, an act of simple domestic service carried out by a spouse as a specific gesture of love. "Look! This offering I give because I love you. See? This thing I do, I do because I love you. To me, you are beautiful, valuable, wonderful. Let me say so. Let me show you."

And just as the child shrieks with joy and embraces the gift-giver, just as the spouse wipes away tears as they read the love letter and lean into their lover's arms, the God of eternal loving relationship—forever dancing in divine love, Father, Son, and Holy Spirit—leans in, draws near, opens his arms, responds.

Yahweh is not a sad, shallow demiurge who demands genuflected minions to rouse his sense of self-importance. He is the God of love, and worship is the exchange of love elevated by the fact that the recipient of our love is both the God over all and the origin and source of all love. When we begin to open our hearts and minds to the story of God, to his immediacy and presence, to his staggering goodness, we are drawn to some means of expressing what we find there.

The practice of that expression creates relational intimacy, stewards closeness, and reshapes our understanding of ourselves and others. Proximity to God is a light that reconfigures our entire being, a spiritual photosynthesis. Worship creates space in the otherwise crowded ebb and flow of our lives to experience the ever-present availability of that proximity and to be changed.

SILENCE

Where worship is active, expressive, often imbued with sound and vision and sensation, the practice of *wilderness* is quiet and still. One wonders what can be accomplished when one is quiet and still, but silence defies accomplishment. It is the learned art of entering into God's presence and embodying the non-performative self. Here, there is nothing that must be said or done or achieved other than time spent. It is the work of becoming like the elderly husband and wife who sit shoulder to shoulder in the quiet of morning, their love passing silently between the two of them again and again. And unlike silent meditation practiced by those beholden to other masters and gods, this practice of wilderness, for the disciple of Jesus, is never an emptying of the consciousness or voiding of the mind. In silence, the apprentice *fills* their mind with the love of God, saturating themselves in his nearness, bringing their awareness constantly to his indwelling presence and staying there. Quietly. Silently.

IV. EVOLUTION OF THE LIZARD BRAIN AND BODY

THE HUMAN BRAIN IS a tangled snarl of contradictory chaos. A supercomputer of divine design, the mind receives and processes external stimuli, generates its own unique pulses and patterns, and steers the happy or hapless soul. The mind configures and reconfigures its own wiring and makeup according to habits, behaviors, and exposures to which it is subjected by the body and soul, which, together with the mind, make up the human triptych.

You are changed by the things you ponder and ingest. It's inevitable. As the body is altered by the things it consumes, so too the mind. All the things to which we devote our attention are capable of changing us, for better or for worse. Gradually, and over time. Screens, mantras, headlines, stories, sitcoms, and songs are all imbued with transformative power, for better or for worse.

Some of the brain input we are subjected to is beyond our specific choosing. It grows from the soil of our environment and upbringing and presuppositions. A lot of what shapes our minds (and souls) we ingest by predisposition, by habit, by primordial tendency. One person prefers coffee; another, tea. One person is drawn to all things melancholy; another, politics; someone else, competition. We feed our mind according to its appetites, and it becomes what it consumes. The person we are (and the person we are becoming) is a result of all we've fed it and of all the things we've done and that have been done to us, what we've experienced and processed—consciously and subconsciously. You are what you eat.

The master's teachings cannot be put into practice, let alone mastered, without simultaneously reshaping the patterns and problems of the mind. The apprentice sets about that work in the following ways.

STUDY

The library of meditation literature we call the Bible is a volume designed for lifelong formational reading and rereading, but its incredible literary sophistication also requires devoted study.

To study the Scriptures is not to resolve them but to better comprehend their many layers of meaning. The story of God was breathed out by his Spirit and committed to scrolls by the authors he inspired in times long past, cultures that no longer exist, languages no longer common. To uncover the inexhaustible beauties partially obscured by these mysteries, the apprentice requires translations, interpretations, context, and authorial intent. In the world of our reading—centuries removed from the original text—all these things are varied, plentiful, and readily accessible: sermons, written works, commentaries, recordings, historical sources, and lexicons.

In the ongoing work of study, the discerning apprentice must seek out and rely on voices and resources who affirm the same truth Jesus' apprentices have affirmed for centuries—the Scriptures and the creeds. Our trusted sources for translation, interpretation, and insight must recognize the writings not as an ancient literary artifact only, but also as inspired and authoritative Scripture, breathed out by God.

We are not afraid of ideas that depart from our perspective, and we are not so arrogant as to assume we can never learn from those with whom we disagree, but we hold fast always to the truth. We refuse to compromise it by suggesting it must submit to our preference. We seek the truth of Scripture as its authors intended, not as we might like it to be. To discover and rediscover it, we need trustworthy guides. What we learn about the Scripture in study gives shape to the way we understand the world, ourselves, and God—seizing our hearts and imaginations with the truth to which we dedicate our focus.

LEARNING

The study of Scripture is supplemented by spiritual learning, both of which are accomplished when the apprentice sits humbly beneath the teaching, writing, and wisdom of other apprentices. This receptive posture demonstrates that the apprentice is ever in search of maturity, growth, and formation, and that no apprentice, young or old, inexperienced or seasoned, is fully realized in their union with the master until the renewal of all things. The humility necessary to learn is also the baseline disposition necessary to propel the art of Christianity; it recognizes that discipleship, by design, is always carried out in relationship and communion with other disciples.

The apprentice, eager to learn, organizes their life to accommodate various genres of teaching; they read books about discipleship, they read and listen to teachers, to spiritual directors, and to guides. They seek out mentorship from the living and the dead, in their writings and sermons and lectures, in dialogue, and around dinner tables.

Only the master has all authority. Any spiritual guide, academic, or ostensible sage who contradicts the master's teaching or his delegated authority in the Scriptures is a blind guide. Do not follow them. Entrust your spiritual learning to the family of faith reaching back for centuries and across the world: men and women of all ages and colors and places, broken and imperfect but faithful to the master as the way, the truth, and the life, the only way to the only true God.

The depth of the master's teaching and the literary complexity of the Scriptures necessitate some level of disagreement as to how one best interprets and applies some of their intricacies. These disagreements are realized in unique expressions of worship, different theological systems, distinct traditions and denominations. But nuanced disagreement does not fundamentally divide the family of faith. If anyone claims to be a brother or sister, let them affirm Jesus as lord by holding to the truth of the Scriptures, by never denying or contradicting his teaching, by writing the creeds on their hearts, and by a life that exemplifies the fruit of faithfulness. The apprentice, in his or her ongoing pursuit of learning, must develop the ability to recognize the truth as the master recognizes the truth, to learn and relearn that truth as long as they live.

CHURCH

No apprentice can realize or accomplish their apprenticeship alone. It is (and always has been) a communal way of life. The apprentice who claims they will follow the master on their own, who will shirk the systems and structures of the church, is blinded by pride. The one who wags their finger at the failings of organized religion refuses to acknowledge the same darkness that dwells within them and raises themselves up above others on the flimsy stilts of their own perceived superiority. Any place where humans gather—be it organic or institutional—will know brokenness, corruption, and failure. The church is no different. But those who submit themselves to the vulnerability and accountability of shared life and discipleship acknowledge both their brokenness and their need for others.

The one who rebuffs the disciplined consistency of church rhythms in order to pursue "spontaneous" spirituality at their own discretion is like a would-be musician who believes they will become a concert pianist by way of occasional tinkering and wishful thinking. All the master's teachings must be carried out within the context of relationships. The church is the consistent, disciplined community rhythm that submits one's life to the love, guidance, correction, and even failure of other apprentices. For if we are unwilling to carry, correct, and forgive the sin of others, who can we expect to do the same for us?

THE BODY

The naturalists say that the body and the brain are all we are. The Greeks believed the immaterial soul that pilots the meatsuit of the body was the only meaningful substance of the human being and that the soul went on forever, long after the body had decomposed in the dirt. But in the inspired, authoritative Scriptures, the human being is mind, body, and soul. The soul is meant for the body, and the body for the soul. At the end of the story, both will be raised. In the age to come, those who choose the master will know life—body and soul. Those who reject the master will know death—body and soul.

To neglect the body is to neglect the soul, and vice versa. A veritable avalanche of scientific data correlating mental and physical health acknowledges the truth written in Hebrew poetry thousands of years prior: that God made the human body, that he filled it with the breath of life, and that the human being became a living soul. The material substance of your person is no less you than your consciousness, and your cells and blood and tissue are no less you than your immaterial spirit.

Every apprentice of the master must honor God with their body by thoughtful selection of what the body consumes and by activity that invigorates the body and its functionality. The simple and ancient human discipline of a healthy diet and consistent exercise is a way of life that demonstrates our acknowledgment of what the Scriptures say is true: we are souls, and we are bodies. To show no concern for the body's activity and consumption is akin to neglecting prayer or study—we are formed by what we do and do not do, body and soul.

V. OTHERS

THE WAY OF JESUS cannot be carried out in isolation. To love God and others, one must conduct life with God and others. To conduct life among others is to know both their beauty and their terrible brokenness and to share both dimensions of oneself also. Life with others unfolds within four rungs of connection.

BEYOND THE COMMUNITY

God loves all people without qualification or condition, so every student of the master is called to love all people accordingly. Love for those with whom we have no practical connection and no relational intimacy is realized through practices of justice, generosity, and prayer. We demonstrate love in action through partnering with charitable causes locally and abroad, through the dedication of prayer, resources, and finances to those in need and to organizations and institutions that care for the poor, the marginalized, the sick, and the oppressed. This kind of actualized love applies to all subsequent rungs of connection, and it sometimes presents itself in the form of organic opportunities. But most often it must be sought out and applied in a planned and practical life rhythm, or else it doesn't much happen at all.

OUTER CIRCLE

Life accomplished in the public square inevitably gathers acquaintances. These long lists of connections are typically populated by everyone from neighbors, coworkers, and other parents at your kid's school, to slightly closer social connections and friendships that develop among them. Various needs that appear in the network of these relationships should be honored with the same dignifying love realized beyond the community, but unlike those outside our relational reach, the people within the outer circle warrant unique dignifying attention and priority. The attention we give others—even the simple honor of focused attention in conversation, remembering names, asking about someone's life—reminds us of the image of God in all people and of our constant need to have our attention focused outward rather than on the recursive loop of the self.

COMMUNITY

The inner circle of relationships consists of chosen friendships and families with whom we create disciplined and consistent rhythms for sharing the most intimate details of our lives. This circle of relationships must include the loving concern necessary for the rungs beneath it but is prioritized above both. The inner circle is where authentic vulnerability is given, and loving accountability is received.

Friends are great, but community is something deeper. We choose friends based on shared preferences and compatible personalities: You like what I like; you entertain me. A community can and often does consist of wildly diverging dispositions and tastes but unites in apprenticeship to the master. In sharing life—time, resources, availability, emotional and spiritual energy—one apprentice enriches their connection to the other, creating a bond stronger than that which ties affinity groups and making it possible to open one's self and to treat the infection of secrets. When each apprentice within the community is privy to the victories, failures, sins, struggles, joys, and sorrows of the others, each can adequately and honestly encourage, affirm, and correct at the deepest levels of knowing and being known.

"I see this in you. Well done."

"I see this in you. It isn't right."

"Let me walk with you in joy."

"Let me walk with you in suffering."

GREATEST INTIMACY

The final core of relationship is reserved for the most unique and greatest intimacy among the master's apprentices and is shared between husbands and wives and between parents and children. To enter the greatest intimacy is not a necessary component of personhood or apprenticeship, but for those who choose marriage, or who also choose children, the greatest intimacy is prioritized above all other human relationships. The apprentice who chooses it seeks to give themselves wholly to self-sacrificial love at all times and in every way.

No apprentice is made more worthy or worthwhile in marriage or in bearing and raising children, and not every apprentice can or should choose either. These ways of life, by providence and chaos and circumstance, present themselves to some and not others, are accepted by some and not others, are navigated with grace by fewer still, and are fulfilled without doing harm by no one. They are to be considered with profound spiritual gravity and accepted at the expense of all the love and life the apprentice has to offer, and by the grace of God, even more.

VI. WORK AND REST

EVERY APPRENTICE IS CALLED to a mission, be it swabbing the sores of lepers in Kolkata, singing songs, teaching algebra, or arranging baked goods and taking coffee orders. No single vocation is uniquely imbued with inherent social or spiritual superiority, and God calls and appoints each of us to different pieces of a whole. Vocation can be abstract: "I am called to serve the poor"; "I am an artist"; "I build things"; "I raise children." The abstraction of vocation is actualized in specific work: "I operate a soup kitchen to feed those in need"; "I write and record music that challenges and provokes the soul"; "I work for an urban planning committee"; "I provide my sons and daughters with everything necessary to become good men and women who follow the master."

The specific expression of vocation can (and likely will) evolve or change outright across years and seasons of life, but the heart of the vocation is unique to the apprentice's God-given identity and calling. Not everyone is lucky enough to perfectly blend their vocation with their job, but sometimes, the two overlap or are one and the same. The apprentice must learn their unique vocation by:

1. Seeking the broad guidance of the Scriptures and the master's teaching
2. Seeking the unique guidance of the Holy Spirit through prayer and prophecy
3. Assessing their own talents, capabilities, and constitutions
4. Inviting wisdom and guidance from trusted spiritual leaders and from the community and greatest intimacy circles of their personal relationships

Many careers cannot be carried out without disobeying the master. The apprentice is called to, by their work, contribute good to a broken world in ways big and small, not to participate—directly or indirectly—in making the world worse. Work in a broken world is messy, but every apprentice must assess the work they do and count the cost of its complications and contradictions. How can anyone obey the master while participating in systems of injustice and oppression, in the exploitation of people or of creation, in work that compels others to sin, or in responsibilities that might require them to do violence?

The vocation of the apprentice—obediently realized and accomplished—is not the apprentice's identity. No apprentice is fundamentally an artist, or mother, or plumber. The identity of the apprentice is always and unchanging: beloved of God. This identity weathers all storms and suffering, vested deep within us before we knew our vocation or could carry it out, and continues to identify us long after whatever career contribution we have or haven't made is a thing of the past. Whether or not we realize our dream of education or artistry or engineering is, ultimately, beyond our total control, and many before and many after us have been made to relinquish those dreams with tears and broken hearts. But our identity cannot be taken nor renounced.

And just as every apprentice must combat indolence and inactivity with work, the apprentice must also combat any illusion of vocation-as-identity with rest. In rest, the apprentice routinely withdraws from all rhythms and reminders of work and sits in the liberating truth that they are not God. Somewhere, a device is always waiting to chime, but not during rest. Phone calls are silenced, meetings and conversations stilled, outstanding assignments remain outstanding, if only for a while. The world may peck at the window of rest, frantic: "Work remains undone! It calls! Your world will crumble unless you work!" But the world insists on its slow circuit around the sun whether we work or not, so rest.

Work and rest alternate within the dance of life's rhythm and both must be accommodated within each week, month, and year. To realize one's vocation through work is a spiritual discipline, and many of the master's other crucial practices—silence, contemplation, and more—can only be realized in rest.

Work, rest, work, rest.

VII. MONEY

OH, THE TERRIBLE, UGLY complication of money. You need it just to eat food and sleep inside, but the mere presence of it can submerge the soul in bottomless, unsatisfiable want. To cut down the grasping tentacles of greed, materialism, and selfishness, the apprentice must wield their finances as if they were a live virus.

Currency itself is not evil, but loving money is. Money can be used for magnificent good, but only when the apprentice abides one of the master's most difficult teachings: "It's better to give things away than keep them for yourself." The master embodied this teaching unto death. But us? We struggle to comprehend that even a few coins could be better spent on anything but ourselves.

Here is how the apprentice practices the ancient art of financial divestment: First, set for yourself a consistent, recurring time marker—by month or by paycheck. With each recurring appointment, the apprentice assesses all funds to which they lay claim and divides them into categories. One category includes all funds the apprentice will expend on their own needs (rent, electricity, groceries, and the like). The next category consists of all funds the apprentice chooses to devote to their own inessential appetites (possessions, entertainment, luxuries). The final category will go beyond the apprentice altogether. It will be donated to justice causes, given to friends and family in need, used to bless others with spontaneous kindness, and pooled with the generosity of brothers and sisters to support the church.

The sum of Category Three must exceed that of Category Two. *It's better to give things away than keep them for yourself.* Spiritual discipline requires more than good intention and does not wait for the slow, unpredictable presentation of serendipitous opportunities to do good, and the formational power of money and possessions—or else generosity—is swift and aggressive. The apprentice must demonstrate by consistent, quantifiable means their determination to be set free from the entangling black vine of money by hacking it as it grows, accepting that which is necessary to live, narrowing that which is selfishly expended, and piling up the offering made in generosity.

All this is done for the sake of others and for the sake of the one who gives. One can only be free from the corrupting power of excess by practicing the art of giving it away.

VIII. GOOD NEWS

HOW DOES THE APPRENTICE share this beautiful thing they have found? For centuries, those who claim the master and his teaching have struggled to answer this question. More than two thousand years ago, the master issued this plain instruction: "Go and make more apprentices. Teach them to obey the things I have taught." And for every moment after, the world has been made to grapple with everything he said and whether or not they will accept it as true.

The master has allowed no recourse other than to accept him as king or renounce him as a liar. The world, however, is unkind to absolutes. They would prefer—much prefer—an ambiguous spectrum, forever subject to the interpretation and implementation of the individual and the individual's unique sensibilities.

Some will say, then, "The master is a fine teacher, I suppose. But he is not king." But the master will not allow for this contradiction; he claimed to be king. Others will say, "I like some of the things the master said, but I do not accept some other things he said." But the master has allowed for no such subjectivity. Either the master speaks all truth, or he speaks only lies. Still others will insist, "I like the master, but I do not like the Scriptures." But the master insisted on them, and the Scriptures contain the master's teaching. There can be no obedience to the master that does not also obey the Scriptures.

His great, jarring, divisive, beautiful, heartbreaking, earth-shattering, life-changing good news rings out across every man, woman, and child, inviting all of us into this great, towering absolute: either he will be to us master, or he will be to us nothing.

This is the invitation he gave us and that we in turn extend with shaking hands to others: come and die. How can we say such a thing to a world unprepared to receive it? Across generations, sincere and false apprentices alike have dressed up strategies and clever covert techniques that make targets of the unconverted, plotting a corkboard map of Polaroids and red thread to ensure the target is most supple, most vulnerable to this very good news. Or, frustrated by the slowness of pamphlets and programs, some rush to shock and sensationalism, painting angry red letters about hell and the apocalypse on sandwich boards and lawn placards. Read and repent, or else.

Terrified of its divisive power and made cautious by centuries of bad practice, many of the master's apprentices would prefer not to say anything at all. They say, "Let them see by our lives! They will behold all the good we do, the peace we carry, and they will *intuit* the good news"—somehow, as if the master's name, claims, and teachings are things that occur to someone from the simple passive act of beholding a good deed.

No, the truth must be spoken and lived, lived and spoken. To the one who follows the master, who listens for the voice of his Spirit, always guiding, always directing, all of life becomes punctuated by invitations to live and speak the truth. Maybe his Spirit will conduct you to a stranger in a supermarket aisle—a momentary interaction that comes and goes, with outcomes the apprentice may never know. Maybe the Spirit will impress upon your heart a person, a group of people, and call you to live and speak, live and speak, again and again for days, months, years. And maybe they will see your life and hear your words and accept both and proclaim the master as king. Or maybe not.

The terrible tragedy of hope *for* the broken is that it must be given *by* the broken. Every quivering apprentice who looks into the eyes of someone who does not yet know the master and, heart laid bare, says, "Here is this beautiful thing I have found!" makes themselves vulnerable to the charge of hypocrisy.

"But you," the lost person might say, "you do not obey your master. Not always. You claim a hope you do not embody without failure. Some of your master's teachings you accept gladly while others you pretend not to hear. How beautiful can this beautiful thing really be if you carry it broken down and bleeding, always falling and failing?"

Then, let the apprentice answer, "Can't you see? The beauty of this beautiful thing cannot be understood only in terms of failure and success. It cannot be evaluated and assessed by its power to produce good behavior or in the consistency of those who hold and carry it. This beautiful thing is made more beautiful by my falling and failing, for it remains forever untarnished by either. Can't you see? This beautiful thing is not a program, not a weekend retreat, not a self-help seminar. This beautiful thing is a love story; my Father in heaven loves me. Because he loves me, because he gives himself up for me in love, he is trustworthy and good. Because he is trustworthy and good, I choose to believe everything he says and to live according to the author of life himself. Because he is trustworthy and good, I accept him. I submit to his way. I kneel before the awesome, fiery power of his invincible love.

"Come and see. I'll go with you."

IX. RESURGAM

YOU ARE GOING TO die. At least once. Maybe more. In the story of the Scriptures, some of how this works is explained with stark, sobering simplicity—all of us die; all of us are raised again; all of us are judged; all of us accept a second, eternal fate in accordance with whether or not we choose to accept the master's invitation to life. This judging and eternity have yet to take place. Both are set somewhere on the timeline of the universe, and no one apart from God knows if that date is days or eons away. Despite its inherent unknowability, many become terribly preoccupied with its specifics. They go looking for codes and clues and herald its imminence again and again, undeterred by a constant string of false alarms. What happens to the dead between dying and the time when they are judged and confront eternity is mysterious. Some theologians interpret certain passages of Scripture to say the dead are in a kind of sleep as they await resurrection. Others, citing the Scripture's promise that to be absent from the body is to be present with God, insist on a kind of soul-consciousness wholly present to

God himself, even in waiting. Maybe they're both right. The only people who know aren't around to tell us about it.

Self-proclaimed Christians have famously emphasized the end of the story to the point of eclipsing the present. In this line of thinking, every mention of "eternal life" from the master refers to something that happens later. Hope is always and only for the future. The beauty of the master and his teaching, they insist, has mostly to do with something that hasn't happened yet but will at some point—when, we don't know.

In an effort to assuage apocalyptic misgivings, other apprentices rightly emphasize the present but often at the expense of the future. The hope of the master, they rebut, is hope for today, and this is also true. But the hope of the master is also in a coming day, somewhere on the horizon, at the resurrection and renewal of all things.

Understanding this, the master's apprentices should look to the future not with anxious hellfire hysteria, but with faith, trust, and hope. The master is going to redeem what's broken, including us.

Death is the awful black blanket that is eventually pulled over every person, whether they're wonderful or terrible or something in between. Death imposes itself on and violates the young and the old with chaotic indifference. It extends its skeletal digit and touches an infant so that cancer blossoms in its lissome bones.

It breathes on young mothers, and aneurysms rupture in their brains. It leans over the old and infirm and draws their eyelids downward like final curtains, never to be raised again. It flicks carelessly at one car so that it barrels into another, and a happy family drive becomes a journey the family will never complete.

Because death skulks phantomlike along the timeline of our lives, able to appear unwelcome and unannounced, the apprentice must learn to live aware and unafraid. Hope waits beyond the shadow of death. We fear no evil, for he is with us.

The apprentice believes in a story that outlasts death—in a cosmos awaiting redemption. All of us die, but the story does not end in death. All of us stand before the master, and to all of us the master extends the gift of life. Some of us, though we are marred by a broken world teetering on death's doorstep, we reach up with trembling hands and accept his gift freely given. We want to know him and be known by him. One day, on the other side of death, we will stand before the master, and though every terrible secret thing will be made known, and though we will give an account for the things we have said and done prior to dying, the master will know us—he who has made his home with us in love. And we will be with him, and he will be with us. And the time of grief and broken things will come to an end.

Others will look on the master's extended hand and scowl. Who is this one so arrogant that he claims to be the way, the truth, and the life? Who is this man of such audacity that he claims to be the only way to God? They will push his hand away. No, thank you. Perhaps I might consider some of your words, the ones I like. But I will not have all of you. No, I am afraid your reputation has been damaged beyond repair by my parents and pastors, by politicians and spiritual leaders who have fallen from grace. I will find God my own way, and it will not be at the end of your narrow road. I will seek out other gods with other names on other roads, and all who take up with you will be exposed as fools and fanatics. What a pity!

The master will not impose himself or his love or his teaching on anyone. Love cannot be imposed. The master does not manipulate nor coerce. The master seeks, pursues, calls out, knocks on the closed door and the shuttered window. The master woos.

And the one who spurns the master's love will not be bent to do otherwise. And if the master's love is true life, to choose other than his love is true death. Again and again, the word the Scriptures use to describe such a fate is *destruction*. I can think of no word better.

Life and death are two doors through which the apprentice—and every human—must pass. Again and again, they choose a door, each entry and exit revealing a new series of corresponding consequences, new paths, another door. But God is always going before them to provide a doorway to life, an escape hatch from death. Two choices. Two doors. Choose life, he pleads. Again and again and again. Choose life.

END OF DEATH

WHAT I WANTED MOST, all my life, I did not know—not really, anyway—until one summer afternoon when I was forty years old. I had been reading and was alone with my thoughts for a moment when it occurred to me, as if from nowhere, that what I wanted most all my life was to be known and to be loved. All these other expressions of want, all my performative flapping and flailing, even the way I wrote and made things, were bids at love. Like all people, like every person, I wanted to be known and loved. And in all my scrambling lifelong desperation for uniqueness, imagine my terrible surprise at admitting to myself that I was just like everyone else after all.

But it occurred to me in that same moment, one thought after the other, that the thing I wanted most was also the only thing I had always had. I had been known and loved by my Father in heaven, who knit me together in my mother's womb and whose goodness and love followed me all the days of my life despite my many prolonged attempts at escaping or hiding from them, or pretending that they weren't there. None of these things, to my great relief, proved effective.

But I was also known and loved by others. At least one of them saw every possible shadow of my soul and resolved to love me anyway. My children loved me without qualification or condition or pretense, as if they had no other choice. Their love changed me.

Though I did not deserve it, there were others to love me as well. Lots of them. But because, for more than three decades, I did not love or even like myself, I would not allow myself to receive much of the love I was given. When I was handed love, I would lunge backward, an evasive maneuver, then examine the love on offer so that I could prepare an explanation for myself as to why I could not receive this love for what it was. When given the thing I wanted most, I would explain it away, always afraid that it was too good to be true.

But that was what seems like a long time ago. Now, having been delivered from my self-loathing, I can see myself for who I am and who I always have been: beloved of God. Now I can see, with neither false modesty nor self-hatred, but rather, relaxed and peaceful (if not perplexed) self-awareness, that though he should probably not love me, he does anyway. Forever and always, he loves me. His love silences despair and smothers the void.

Forever and always, he loves me.

For as long as I can remember, I've written about death and dying. I've written songs and books and sermons about them. I've spoken at funerals and pastored the grieving. Aside from the great impassive majesty and mystery of it, I'm not sure why I often think about death when I write. Maybe it's for me. Maybe it's for you.

All of living is a series of deaths. All of us endure these deaths—each of them after the other—and we become something other than what we were before we died. People like me write about the inevitability of death in part because we are convinced that the world wants badly to pretend it isn't so, and such a charade is foolhardy. But maybe people like me write and talk about death—that it's coming, maybe very soon—because it scares us.

The thing that scares me more than any other thing isn't spiders or shark attacks or environmental collapse. I am most afraid of meaninglessness. Maybe in our own ways, all of us are. I am afraid that if, after writing these words, I step outside and a boulder falls on my head and crushes my skull, my wife will find a new husband, my children will find a new dad, my loved ones will find a new friend. I am afraid that all the places I once populated with great meaning, after being temporarily vacated, will be refilled. I am afraid of a world that would be the same without me in it or even better for my absence.

Because if I disappear, and if the once white-hot love reserved for me and all the little twirling special artifacts of my person have nowhere else to go but into the fog of memory, I worry that it will burn up or go to someone else. I worry that I will become a shelved legend of sorts, a character once loved but long gone. I worry that all the tangles and disfigurements of my person will be smoothed out into a palatable story to be recalled on appropriate occasions but otherwise forgotten. I worry that any passion or desire once reserved for me will be redirected, that it was just a feeling that had to go somewhere and that I happened to be where it landed for a little while. I worry that when I'm gone, anything of real substance that made me *me* will be gone too. Then it will be as if I was never known or loved at all.

But maybe every gibbering mouthpiece of death, like me, can learn to speak as often and more so about the great unstoppable inevitability of love. People like me are afraid to concede to the superior power of love because we are afraid it is not for us, but it is. People like me are worried that, if we extol the great and glorious scope of love, we might wear it out or make it cheap, as if love—in the truest sense—is at all subject to wear and tear or that it can be thinned by exposure or spoiled by time.

Love originates in God, who is more than the author of love, but who *is* love himself. All of our imperfect human approximations of love are mere reflections of the one true God who is love. If the most effortlessly self-sacrificial love in all the world between a parent and a child were a matchstick, the love of God for people is a supernova. This is something that people like me are afraid to believe. To *really* believe, I mean.

We lift the back of our hands before our terrified gaze, and we squint between fanned fingers, saying, No, wait, this love would not burn so bright if it knew me. But it does. And it goes on burning. Brighter and brighter, it burns. And we scramble backward, arms folded over our ducked heads in an attempt to hide our own perceived ugliness—as if any part of us could be hidden—and we reason with the nuclear blast of love, "Wait, such love cannot shine on me!" But it does. Illuminating and radiating us. Burning us up.

For years and years, I cowered before the light of love, my face in my hands, assuring myself and the one in whom love originates that there were very good reasons indeed for my hiding away from it. But then one arm fell to my side. And then the other. And slowly, carefully, I opened my eyes and let love in. I let love in.

I wish I could say my struggle against love came to some conclusive end then, but it did not. Dying—the kind of dying that matters most—is the ongoing process of surrendering to love.

This kind of dying acts as a doorway to life and not the other way around. Each time I find the door, I step through it and look for it again. Sometimes, I run from one to the other as if weightless. Alive with joy. Sometimes, I hobble, blood-sodden and empurpled by the wounds of foolishness and sin, and my gaze strains through swollen lids for the next door and then the next. All of living is a series of deaths, but death is not the end.

The dance of doors comes to an end eventually. Here, there is no longer any death to be found and accomplished. Here, all our dying is made complete in love. Everything we wanted and hoped for—everything that ever really mattered—is resolved in love. Love is the end of death.

Here, the thing that scares me most is a fiction. An imaginary monster from a storybook and nothing more. And then his arms are around me, and the idea that I might be anything other than known and loved is revealed for the absurdity it always was. And I realize both of us are laughing. I'm still laughing when he wipes away the last of my tears. The very last tears I'll ever shed.

DISCIPLE'S VOW

I am a disciple of Christ.
I will not compromise.
I will keep his teaching ever before me.
I will keep his commands because I love him.
I will write them on my heart.
He is with me always, even until the end of the age.

All of life's troubles and all the fury of hell
will not stop me from loving him.
The Liar will not lead me astray.
I defy him.
I refuse to be sated by a dominion of death.
Jesus is lord, forever.

Amen.

FINAL PARABLE: THE IDIOT SON

THIS IS HOW I finally decided to leave home. I woke up one morning and realized none of it mattered to me, not really. I remember looking around my bedroom, around my father's mansion, and realizing how meaningless everything was. Yeah, he was very rich, my father, but it was his, not mine. All of it. People talked about my father's generosity, but I never felt like it was worth mentioning. I walked the halls of his house looking at things, turning expensive-looking vases upside down to see if anything fell out of them. Nothing ever did. Figures. That's what I remember thinking, looking out the window at all the hired help milling about the grounds, smiling, laughing together, contented with some small stewardship of someone else's fortune. None of us had anything. Only my father. That's when I decided to leave.

My brother, he had it in for me from the beginning. He was like the hired help: unquestioning in his dumb loyalty, contented to have nothing. He was there when I said I was leaving, scowling his disapproval from the other side of the dinner table, the three of us in our father's ridiculous dining room. My brother was so like one of my father's servants: consistent. I was the inconsistency. I wanted out. That's how I put it when I asked for the money. To me, it made perfect sense.

I said to my father, "Haven't you allocated our inheritance already?"

He said that he had.

I told him, "Well, who knows when and if that inheritance will find its way to us? Why not dole it out now and let me go make my own way? And, really, what future is there here for a son—cooped up in your estate with no life of my own?"

When I said this, I saw something move across my father's face. Disappointment. When I saw it, I was as ready to go as I'd ever been. He was so selfish, my father. Never happy with me or with anything I ever did. Here I was, practically groveling at his feet for what was rightfully mine. Why should I have to reason and plead, other than him making a show of his power? But then, before I could tell him what I really thought about it, he said, "Okay."

"Okay?"

"Okay, if that's what you want. You're not a prisoner here."

And that was that. His people wrote the check and made the deposit. Part of me wondered if my brother would get a clue then, that he'd see another life for himself without our father, but he stayed. His face the same frozen glower from the time I'd asked for my inheritance to the moment I packed the last of my things and left for the city. *Good riddance*, I thought.

It was good being in the city. My new friends kept talking about all the money I had. I bought a loft and a car, but basically, I was responsible with it. "It's so much money," they'd say, but it wasn't. "He barely gave me anything," I said. "He's a selfish cheapskate," I said. All I'd ever been able to do was what my father let me do. Before, I could only eat the food he prepared, but in the city, I could eat whatever I wanted to eat, and I realized then that my appetites had mutated, made desperate and groaning by all that my father had withheld. Without his constant, towering disapproval clouding my judgment, I was able to open my mind and my senses and enjoy life without fear of judgment or reproof. I did what I wanted to do, and doing what I wanted to do made me happy. Really happy. I could finally see, touch, taste, and enjoy all the kinds of things I'd been led to believe would do me harm. I could see these doomsday prophecies of certain death as little more than attempts at control, and I was grateful to have cast them off and be rid of them for good.

My system was constantly flooded with dopamine. I ingested the kinds of chemicals and experiences, the foods and drinks and substances my father had—in his puritanical obsession with control—kept from me. I thought of him sometimes, my father, of the way his brow furrowed when I'd told him I was leaving, the way tears gathered in the creases of his old face. He could never just let me be happy. I guess I missed him sometimes. There were moments, brief but disconcerting, usually when the drug haze subsided or after I'd pulled myself away from some sweating, writhing body in my bed, when a kind of dull ache set in, distant but palpable. A vague dread. But then a numbness would settle over me, cloudlike and cooling, and rather than relief, I didn't feel much of anything at all. Feeling nothing was better sometimes.

It had been several seasons before I allowed myself to confront the reality of my declining funds. I went looking for work for the first time but found none. People kept talking about some recession settling into the city's economic framework. People were losing jobs. No one was hiring. This was only temporary, people were saying. "It'll turn around," they said. "Soon," they said.

My anxiety was threatening to evolve into full-blown hysteria. To keep it quiet, I fed it more of the things it liked to eat, reasoning that if I slowed down, even just a little, I could ration my remaining resources and survive the drought. It didn't work. My father's selfishness was my undoing. My inheritance, in the end, his "generous" provision became another one of his many attempts to sabotage me—enough to taste independence but not enough to sustain it. Various withdrawals set in, and there wasn't enough money for the kind of drugs or sex to which I had become accustomed. I realized too late that I preferred both to food and shelter, and as such, I lost all four.

The old man who settled my eviction directed me to a shelter for junkies and bums, but I was neither, so I declined. He then offered me a day-labor gig removing the garbage accumulating in the city streets and alleys due to budget cuts and strikes or some such thing. Nothing about handling garbage excited or interested me. It wasn't a role that made any sense for someone like me, and they weren't paying enough for it to be done either way. But there was a terrible pain in my stomach now and something like an itch in my brain, and if I trudged through the trash work, I could relieve both by night, so that's what I did.

I lost weight. My eyes seemed to sink in their sockets, the thin skin encircling them going grey. The other trash grunts said I looked sickly. They'd get frustrated, saying I was too slow, too weak. I guess I wasn't eating as much as I was supposed to. It was getting harder to accomplish the daily exchange of a day's wages for the things I needed to survive the night. I pushed myself to endure the early hours just to get to the part where I could forget everything leading up to that moment, but every time I completed the cycle of working and forgetting, it got harder to wake up at all. When the weather changed, I gave in and went to the shelter for junkies and threw up.

The next morning, I went to gather a bulging sack of refuse from an alley behind an apartment building, and the shining black plastic split as I lifted it, the bag yawning open and vomiting its contents onto the hot cement, pooling around my ankles. There were paper towels and empty cereal boxes, coffee grounds and banana peels. Without thinking, I reached for the peels, unfolding them carefully, ape-like, looking for any abandoned or partially eaten fruit, but finding only decay. Flies swirled around my head. For the first time in a long time, I thought about my father.

I imagined his employees in their comfortable little homes, eating their satisfying little dinners. I was flushed with a momentary anger, but, to my surprise, it faded. I was tired. I blinked tears from my eyes and looked up from the garbage heap. I could see with a kind of pale clarity that I had so willfully distanced myself from sonship that whatever familial connection had once existed between my father and me had been erased by everything I said and did. There was a weight on me then, unbearable and crushing, and I wanted to disappear beneath it. I considered this for a moment and realized that what I wanted more—what I wanted most—was to go home. I looked out on the city skyline and thought of what I might say when I saw him. If I saw him. My head fell on the thin stalk of my neck, and I breathed deep the smell of soiled diapers and stale cigarettes. I thought of the tears on my father's face, and I whispered these words to myself as I thought them: "Father, I was wrong. I know that I can't come home, that I can't be your son anymore. I don't deserve anything from you. But can I have a job? Any job. I'll stay out of your way and work quietly. You don't owe me anything. I don't want to die all by myself."

I said all those things to myself, then I took a deep breath and decided to go home. I half-suspected the days on the road—the long walks and chaotic zigzag of hitchhiking—would eventually discourage my homecoming. Instead, I found myself staring out of truck beds and across long expanses of highway, thinking the words to myself again and again, my lips moving silently as I rehearsed them, the words solidifying somewhere inside me.

The stomach pain began during the final hours of the journey, and I opted to walk the final few miles in order to gather myself and my prepared speech. I was seized again by a terrible, debilitating shame. The image of my father's face, twisted by disgust, flashed in my mind, and I stopped walking and stood still. I wanted badly to abandon the effort of it all but could think of nothing else to do with myself, so I kept walking and mumbling, nauseous and trembling, as my father's estate appeared in the distance. I was quaking then, stuttering, fumbling the words as I whispered, a breathy prayer that kept me from collapsing.

Before I'd gotten much closer, a figure appeared in the distance and grew. A man running toward me. I slowed, anxious and bleary-eyed, and watched the figure as it barreled forward. He was maybe fifty feet away when I realized it was my father.

I was taking rapid, shallow breaths, terrified. I stopped walking and mumbled the words to myself once more, worried I'd lose them, attempting to steel myself against his inevitable rejection. Had he seen me from his window and come to send me away? Would he not even hear my plea for mercy? Then he was in front of me, and I could see the same tears in the lines of his face, inches away. Anger? Disappointment? Then he threw his arms around me and kissed my face, sobbing. Panicked and aghast, I babbled my prepared monologue, an anxious reflex. "Father," I said, "I was wrong. I know I can't be your son anymore . . ." Then, there were other figures running forward, all of them smiling. My father, ignoring my speech, called to them, "He's home!" There was something in his voice. Not anger nor disappointment. It was relief. Joy. "He's home, he's home," my father kept saying, weeping unashamedly. "Hurry! He's shivering! Bring him a coat. Everyone drop what you're doing. Tonight, we celebrate!" And he wouldn't release me from his embrace. He kissed me again and again. "You're home," he said to me, just me, quietly in my ear, his voice shuddering, his great body heaving, his strong arms around me. "Oh my son. My beloved son. You're home."

All night I was surrounded by smiling faces, hands on my shoulders, arms around me. "Welcome home!" everyone kept saying. I floated through the festivities in disbelief. Part of me wanted to shrink until I became invisible, but there was such sincerity in their eyes and such gentleness in their touch that I couldn't help but relent and stand helpless before the light of love, burning and restorative. I was, of course, humiliated by my seasons in the city, but no one used them against me. My dad wouldn't let me out of his sight. I was a little boy before him.

I tried once or twice more to offer my speech, but the music of celebration and the cries of excitement always interrupted me. I thought them once more, *Father, I was wrong. I know that I can't come home* . . . But I could and I did. *I know I can't be your son anymore* . . . But that was the only thing he'd called me since the moment he came running: "My son. My beloved son." So, I gave up on saying it. I realized that all along my long journey home, I'd become entirely convinced that the mere sight of me would aggravate years of bitterness and disgust in my dad and everyone who belonged to his household, but the only thing anyone seemed to care about was that I'd been gone and now I was home. I was a stupid sheep that wandered into a dark wood and got lost, but his love found me and brought me home. Even with so much else within his vast dominion, he came running for me.

As the party carried on without slowing, my brother appeared in a distant doorway, framed by the darkness beyond. He was surrounded by the eager and excited, beckoning him into the celebration, but he would not oblige them. My dad went to him, and I watched the two of them in silent conversation. He looked at my brother the way he'd looked at me, with patience and compassion. But why? My brother had not wandered as I had. I stood and went to reassure my brother but stopped short when I could hear the indignation in his voice.

"Why do you celebrate your idiot son?" my brother asked. "Where is my party? I've never compromised, never left, never disobeyed you. Every day, I've worked for you. I've accomplished every chore, obliged every routine. My brother, the one who dedicated the gift of his inheritance to hookers, this is who you choose to reward? To celebrate?"

I watched as my dad took my brother's face in his hands. He said to him, "My son. Your home is with me." He swept an arm through the air, gesturing at the celebrating throng, at the vastness of it. "All of this belongs to you," my dad told my brother. "Everything. But your brother came home, son. How could we not celebrate?"

EPILOGUE: HOW TO DIE

EVERY MONTH I DRIVE to a monastery at the top of a hill. Where I live, for most of the year, it rains. The rain comes in thin sheets, like white noise against the monks' windswept robes as they pass me on their way to afternoon prayer. All around the monastery hangs the image of Jesus on the cross. In sculptures, paintings, and icons, he hangs. In the library, the chapel, the visitor's center, he hangs. On one such cross, the head of Jesus is bent low by gravity, his neck useless in death. Of course, these are only visual representations of a past reality. Jesus no longer hangs on the cross nor sleeps in the tomb. And yet, Jesus—as he is now, alive, not as he was then, dying or dead—occupies every square inch of that monastery. In the library, he stands. In the chapel and visitor center, he stands. Down the road that leads out of the monastery, he stands. In the nearby town, he stands. Everywhere in all the world, Jesus stands as if before a door.

"Here I am!" he announces again and again. "I stand at the door and knock. If anyone hears my voice and opens the door, I will come in and be with that person, and they with me."

Every month, I visit a monastery at the top of a hill. I watch the monks pass in their long black robes, and I think about the monks before them and the ones before those monks, reaching back across centuries. These monks, before they donned robes and rosaries, left life as they once knew it. They forfeited sex and possessions and made vows to God and one another. For them, life became *ora et labora*: "pray and work." It's a big commitment, being a monk. A kind of dying.

Monks, like all humans, get it wrong sometimes. Some of them crawl into dark caves and chain themselves to stones. The robed and religious, like the unrobed and irreligious, can accomplish all manner of foolishness and evil. But because they are robed, because they were to devote themselves to prayer and work, their failures become the scandals—the terrible hypocrisy—that unseat the religious imagination. Frauds, we think. They and their God.

But though humans can and should be held accountable for the things they say and do—and though the heart and soul of a human being are revealed in what they say and do, how they live—all human beings are, at times, a nervous bundle of contradictions and paradoxes. Most of us want good but do evil. And even those who claim to carry out evil with purpose and intention, somewhere within them the skeleton reaches out for good—for the *something* behind and beyond all this. And some of these walking contradictions, these scoundrels and fools and hypocrites, they discover a seam in the veil that separates all we see from all we don't, and the seam splits, and the veil falls, and, beholden to what lies beyond the veil, they are changed. They strain up and out of the split exoskeleton, a kind of dying.

Christians, like Christ, have been dying for a long time. At one time, in the ancient Near East, people threw stones at Christians until their bones snapped and their skulls ruptured and their organs burst. They set Christians in fiery furnaces and watched their skin bubble and peel. They impaled Christians on spears and burned them on stakes. In Lebanon, they slit throats and stabbed hearts. In Indonesia, they disemboweled Christians with machetes. In the Philippines, they were beheaded with an axe. There were fires in England and bullets in Cuba, in China, in America. In North Korea, Christians have been flattened by steamrollers. In Egypt, their flesh was raked away with steel combs. I think about these Christians sometimes. Some of them said and did incredible things in the midst of their torture and execution. They sang hymns or quoted Scripture or prayed forgiveness for their executioners. Like Jesus.

A lot like Jesus, actually.

For centuries, all over the world, men and women of all nationalities and ethnicities and ages and traditions have set aside the life they lived before Jesus found them and saved them and took up his life instead. This is my story too. The story I want to live.

One morning at that monastery on the top of the hill, I sat on a bench watching the rain. I was praying. I saw in my mind a vision of worship—all manner of disciples across time caught up in celebration, enraptured. There were those mauled to death by lions as a punishment for their refusal to denounce Jesus, those run through by Roman swords or shot or skewered or dismembered or beheaded or flayed alive. And then there were scores of less remarkable disciples, like me, who mostly lived on quiet streets, typed in offices, walked their kids to school, visited monasteries once a month. I was there among them. So was my wife. So were my children. My daughter, who was seven that morning, could hardly breathe when she saw Jesus. My firstborn son, who was ten, wept. Even though he couldn't explain why, I knew. Even my youngest child, who was only two, was there in my vision. I hoisted him up on my shoulders so he could see over the joyous host of holy women and holy men, so that he could see Jesus. His eyes went wide when he saw him. In his smallness, he understood immediately something the bigger among us forget and must relearn over a lifetime and longer. Some of us never do.

I sat on that bench praying. Listening. And Jesus sat beside me, no longer confined to the cross that held him for such a brief moment in history two thousand years prior, before he left it and the grave and death behind forever. He sat on the bench, he walked the halls of the library, the chapel, the visitor's center, as if before a door.

Look! He stands before you as you read, as you listen. He looks at you, and he smiles. The way he did in the beginning when his Spirit hovered over the waters. The way he did when he knit you together in your mother's womb. He stands now, smiling, as if before a door. "Here I am!" he says. "I stand at the door and knock. If you hear my voice and open the door, I will come in and be with you, and you with me." Can you hear him knocking?

Listen. Listen.

"THEREFORE EVERYONE WHO HEARS THESE WORDS OF MINE AND PUTS THEM INTO PRACTICE IS LIKE A WISE MAN WHO BUILT HIS HOUSE ON THE ROCK. THE RAIN CAME DOWN, THE STREAMS ROSE, AND THE WINDS BLEW AND BEAT AGAINST THAT HOUSE; YET IT DID NOT FALL, BECAUSE IT HAD ITS FOUNDATION ON THE ROCK.

"BUT EVERYONE WHO HEARS THESE WORDS OF MINE AND DOES NOT PUT THEM INTO PRACTICE IS LIKE A FOOLISH MAN WHO BUILT HIS HOUSE ON SAND. THE RAIN CAME DOWN, THE STREAMS ROSE, AND THE WINDS BLEW AND BEAT AGAINST THAT HOUSE, AND IT FELL WITH A GREAT CRASH."

MATTHEW 7:24–27

ACKNOWLEDGMENTS

Thank you to the kind and supportive family of David C Cook, who have bravely welcomed me with open arms. My agent, Amanda Luedeke, has advocated for me and my more unconventional ideas. My gentle and clever editors, Kevin Scott and Leigh Davidson. For my writing on the Sermon on the Mount, I am particularly indebted to the work of Scot McKnight, N. T. Wright, Ben Witherington, Dallas Willard, Stanley Hauerwas, R. T. France, Tim Mackie, Gerry Breshears, and Frederick Dale Bruner. All that is sound is to their credit. Any errors are to mine. The Order of the Tarrasque—including Patrick Porter, Matt Hughes, Gavin Bennet, and Michael Dumont—walk with me in shared life, including the reading and revising of this book. The family of Van City Church, and our staff and leadership— Cameron Silsbee, Levi Warren, Taylor Long, Scott Bargaehr, Tiffany and Kevin Erickson, Jan Lampe, Katie VanDomelen,

Keana Zoradi, Lexi Listek, Josiah Sheffer, Garrett Lane, Matt Johnson, Hannah Brooks, and Tim Wright—have consistently supported me and my writing. Vanessa Porter, Peter and Alla Nikiforov, and Mike and Lindsi Jensen have offered years of community around the dinner table. My children, Beck, Isla, and Arlo, have loved me. Their love is among the most vital of all components of my spiritual formation. My wife, Abigail, has been and will always be second only to the master as my sweetest friend. Thank you.

DAVID C COOK

JOIN US.
SPREAD THE GOSPEL.
CHANGE THE WORLD.

We believe in equipping the local church with Christ-centered resources that empower believers, even in the most challenging places on earth.

We trust that God is *always* at work, in the power of Jesus and the presence of the Holy Spirit, inviting people into relationship with Him.

We are committed to spreading the gospel throughout the world—across villages, cities, and nations. We trust that the Word of God will transform lives and communities by bringing light to the darkness.

As a global ministry with a 150-year legacy, David C Cook is dedicated to this mission. Each time you purchase a resource or donate, you're supporting a ministry—helping spread the gospel, disciple believers, and raise up leaders in some of the world's most underserved regions.

Your support fuels this mission.
Your partnership sends the gospel where it's needed most.

Discover more. Be the difference.
Visit DavidCCook.org/Donate